The Mongols

PAST IMPERFECT

Past Imperfect presents concise critical overviews of the latest research by the world's leading scholars. Subjects cross the full range of fields in the period ca. 400—1500 CE which, in a European context, is known as the Middle Ages. Anyone interested in this period will be enthralled and enlightened by these overviews, written in provocative but accessible language. These affordable paperbacks prove that the era still retains a powerful resonance and impact throughout the world today.

Director and Editor-in-Chief

Simon Forde, *'s-Hertogenbosch*

Production

Ruth Kennedy, *Adelaide*

Cover Design

Martine Maguire-Weltecke, *Dublin*

The Mongols

Timothy May

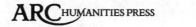

British Library Cataloguing in Publication Data

A catalogue record for this book is available from the British Library

© 2019, Arc Humanities Press, Leeds

ISBN (print): 9781641890946
e-ISBN (PDF): 9781641890953
e-ISBN (EPUB): 9781641890960

www.arc-humanities.org
Printed and bound by CPI Group (UK) Ltd, Croydon, CR0 4YY

Contents

Contents

In memory of Christine Garite

Acknowledgements

This book has been thirty years in the making. Not literally—I write fairly quickly—but the ideas have been percolating in my mind for some time. When Erin T. Dailey approached me about writing a book on the Mongols for the Past Imperfect series, I agreed as long as it was not a straight narrative history. I wanted it to revolve around a question—Why were the Mongols successful? This, of course led to a second question—Why did the Mongol Empire come to an end? Two simple questions that are anything but simple. The first question has been one that has piqued my curiosity since I first became interested in the Mongols. Erin was game and for that I thank him and for all of his help since that initial conversation.

While most of my work has followed other lines, these two questions have always lurked in the background. I make no promise that this book is the final answer—the more I learn about the Mongols, the less I know. I will say, that if nothing else, it should generate some discussion and hopefully among students in a classroom, for whom it is intended.

I would like to thank a number of teachers including Professor Abdul-Karim Rafeq who permitted me to work on the Mongols for an honors thesis at The College of William & Mary and the late Professor Larry W. Moses for his classes and numerous early morning conversations at Indiana University. At the University of Wisconsin, Michael Chamberlain, Anatoly Khazanov, Uli Schamiloglu, and Kemal Karpat pushed me to consider aspects outside of the empire without discouraging my study of the Mongol Empire. David Morgan can never be thanked enough.

Outside of formal academic study, I have had numerous conversations at the Central Eurasian Studies Society conferences, the Mongolia Society, and then various conferences here and there. A number of people have forced me to reconsider ideas or confirmed certain thoughts. There are too many to include, but certain individuals merit distinction due to their questions, answers, and amount of time they endured my conversations. First and foremost to Paul D. Buell with whom I've had a running conversation for twenty years. Christopher P. Atwood, who taught me Mongolian at Indiana, but only more recently joined the Mongol Empire. Scott C. Levi at Ohio State University frequently asks intriguing questions and is always willing to put me in front of high school teachers (who ask even better questions) for NEH workshops. George Lane, Bruno De Nicola, Michal Biran, Anne Broadbridge for their questions, comments, and criticisms over the years. Michael Hope and Simon Forde both read and commented on an early draft. Any errors remain my own. Finally, I thank Reuven Amitai not only for the long conversations and insight on Yiddish terms, but also for the kind words about me he passed to David Morgan when David moved to Wisconsin.

I have kept referencing and citations to the minimum in keeping with the series and the aspiration to make this book as readable as possible.

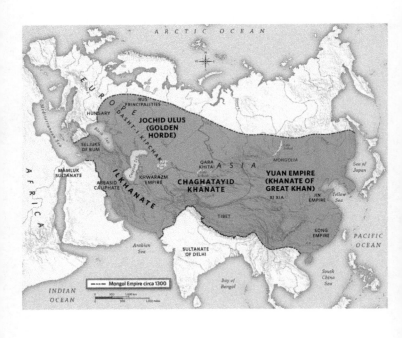

Introduction

It was a dark and stormy night when the Mongol fleets anchored off the coast of Japan at Hakata Bay and Imari Bay in 1281. With their fleet arranged as a floating fortress, the Mongols waited for a dawn that never came as a *tsunami* struck the Mongol fleet, destroying much of the fleet and scattering the remainder. The failure at Japan marked a tipping point for the Mongols. No longer did their armies march inexorably across Eurasia defeating all who opposed them, creating an empire that stretched from the shores of Korea to Bulgaria. Even after the dissolution of the empire in 1260, each of the successor states would be considered a super-power in modern terminology. Yet, the Mongols soon found themselves engaged in desultory civil wars rather than new conquests. How did it reach this point? Considering that the Mongols began their empire as a rather inconsequential power in the steppes of Mongolia, among a half dozen similar groups, another question comes to mind: Why were the Mongols successful in the first place?

Much of the Mongols' success had to do with the appearance of Temüjin, the man who became Chinggis Khan. Before his appearance on the historical stage, the Mongols were but a minor tribe at a time when the Jin Empire (1125–1234) in northern China and Manchuria defeated an ascending Mongol khanate in the 1160s. Temüjin's father, Yesügei died in 1171, poisoned by Tatars, rivals of the Mongols.[1] With the defeat of the Mongols, the Tatars dominated eastern Mongolia. The Tatars were a powerful confederation bordering the Jin Empire, providing better access to trade and wealth. In the past, confederations like the Tatars rose to regional dominance and sometimes even held sway over all of the Mongolian steppes. Yet, the Tatars were not the only powerful tribe in the Mongolian steppes.

In Central Mongolia, the Kereit held sway. Ruled by Toghril Khan, the Kereit had close ties with the Mongols. Toghril had been *anda* or blood brother to Yesügei and became the suzerain of Temüjin. The Kereit, however, controlled the Orkhon Valley, which historically conveyed legitimacy to previous steppe empires.[2] Missionaries from the Church of the East, also known as Nestorians, exerted influence upon the Kereit. Although not all of the Kereit were Nestorians, many of the aristocracy converted. Their conversion to a world religion gave them entry to a wider network through connections along the Silk Road as well as relations with other tribes influenced by the Church of the East such as the Önggüd to the south and the Naiman to the west. Additionally, the Kereit maintained ties with regional powers such as Xi Xia to the south and Qara Khitai to the west, as did the Naiman who were former subjects of Qara Khitai.[3]

Further west and situated on both sides of the Altai Mountains were the Naiman, a Turkic confederation. Through their association with the empire of Qara Khitai, the Naiman also had access to other Nestorians in Central Asia, broadening their cultural vision. Indeed, the Naiman adopted literacy by using the script used by the Uighurs, who were also ruled by Qara Khitai. Unlike the Naiman, the Uighurs were predominantly Buddhists and tended to dwell in the oasis towns of modern Xinjiang. With literacy, contacts to other civilizations and trade routes, the Naiman were positioned to rise in importance. Other smaller tribes such as the Merkit and Önggüd also played a role in the steppes, but the Naiman, Kereit, and Tatars were all better placed to influence history than the Mongols. Yet, larger and well-organized states also existed who were situated to prevent the rise of the Mongols.

Despite being what is today Kazakhstan and Kyrgyzstan, Qara Khitai still exerted influenced in Mongolia. Established in 1125 by Khitan refugees from the Liao Empire (906–1125) in north China, Manchuria, and Mongolia, Qara Khitai was a steppe empire that ruled a population of pagans, Buddhists, Christians, and Muslims. Yelü Dashi (1087–1143), the first Gur-Khan of Qara Khitai, defeated the Seljuq Sultan, Sanjar (r. 1118–1157) in 1141 bringing his borders to the Amu Darya River. The nascent Khwārazmian dynasty (1077–1231), situated south of the Aral Sea, also submitted but remained relatively autonomous. By the thirteenth century, the latter began to assert its own prowess. By not directly challenging the Khitans and using Qara Khitai to secure its northern borders, Khwārazm, ruled by Sultan Muhammad Khwārazmshāh II (1200–1220) expanded into Iran, absorbing Seljuq principalities. He also moved against his primary competition for Iran, the Ghūrid Empire (1186–1206) in Afghanistan. Muhammad even launched an attack against the Abbasid Caliphate (750–1258) in Baghdad. Although it failed, it demonstrated his reach and that Muhammad would not tolerate a resurgent Caliphate in Iran.

East of Qara Khitai sat the Buddhist kingdom of Xi Xia (1038–1227), a poly-ethnic and polyglot realm of nomads, sedentary Turks, and Han Chinese, but ruled by the Buddhist Tangut, a Tibetan people. Dominating the Gansu corridor, a key artery of the Silk Road, Xi Xia was a wealthy realm that at times paid tribute or warred with the Song Empire to the southeast as well as the Jin Empire. Additionally, they forged relations with the polities in the steppes, the Kereit in particular. It was not unusual for Kereit princes who fell out of favour in the steppes to take refuge there.

The Jin Empire (1125–1234), the most powerful entity in East Asia, ruled an empire consisting of North China (extending south to the Huai River) as well as Manchuria, from which the ruling elite came. These were the Jurchen, a Manchurian people who deposed the Liao Empire in 1125. As their dynastic name (Jin) meant Gold, the steppe tribes referred to the Jin Emperor as the Altan Khan or Golden Ruler. While the Jin did not extend their rule into the steppes, as did the Liao, they did meddle in steppe affairs, favouring one tribe over another, creating a delicate balancing act to prevent one tribe from dominating and becoming a threat to the Jin. While steppe confederations had threatened northern China for centuries, it seems unlikely that the Jin were overly concerned—cautious, but not afraid. By the thirteenth century, they not only had a large experienced army, but also seventy-five years' experience in manipulating events in the steppes.

In the far western end of the steppes, the Kipchaks had not coalesced into a coherent body that threatened regional, much less global domination. The Kipchaks were Turkic nomads who arrived in the Pontic and Caspian steppes in the twelfth century, possibly as part of a chain reaction caused by the Liao domination of Mongolia. Known variously as Cumans, Polovtsy, Kipchaks, and Qangli (the eastern branch), they all spoke the same northern Turkic dialect. Rather than forming a single dominant state, they existed in four or five confederations. While sedentary societies such as the Rus' and Khwārazmians fought them, they also formed alliances with various tribes and even inter-married. While a medieval peasant might disagree, in the larger scheme of history, the Kipchaks were a nuisance but not a threat. They proved resilient and difficult for anyone to control over the long term.

Thus in the late-twelfth century and early thirteenth century, there was no obvious reason why the Mongols should became a global power with strong states hemming them in. While in hindsight, it is easy to identify their weaknesses, at the time, there was no reason to suspect that the Mongols would be the wildcard that toppled empires. Among the nomads, no single confederation had emerged from Mongolia in three hundred years to threaten the status quo, much less establish an empire. Even the Tatars and Kereit lacked the gravitas and unity to exert dominion over others.

So what made the Mongols successful? Recently, scientists have argued that wet and cool weather facilitated the rise of the Mongol Empire.[4] The weather was perfect for the steppes, allowing the nomads of Mongolia to flourish. With ample grass, the flocks and herds of the Mongols thrived, permitting them to expand beyond Mongolia. This hypothesis, however, does not explain how the Mongols dominated Mongolia, as other nomads must have benefited from the lush pastures as well. Again, the Mongols were not a significant power at the time of Temüjin's (the man who became Chinggis Khan) birth. While the lush pastures may have aided their outward expansion, climatic reasons fail to explain their initial success.

There are a number of approaches to study the past. One that has fallen out of favour is the Great Man Theory. In this idea, which originated in the nineteenth century, history is explained through reference to the rise and fall of remarkable individuals who possessed sufficient charisma and ability to influence events in a significant and lasting manner.[5] The counter-argument is that all people are shaped by their society; thus social conditions influence events. There is no denying this argument, first formally expressed by Herbert Spencer. Yet Spencer's Social Darwinism or "survival of the fittest" does not adequately explain Chinggis Khan's success.[6] Of course, Herbert Spencer, with his Victorian sensibilities, would not have viewed Chinggis Khan positively in his scheme of progress.[7] Nonetheless, the Great Man (or Woman) Theory still has application. It took a Great Man to propel the Mongols to the forefront of history. Chinggis Khan, however, was not alone in his actions; his generals and advisors were attracted by his personal charisma and seemingly divine favour. There were a number of individuals on the steppe who had similar opportunities to Chinggis Khan, but only he emerged to be remembered as the greatest conqueror in history and the father of Mongolia, while other steppe leaders are only known readily to scholars of the Mongol Empire. Yet we must also restrain our enthusiasm for the Great Man Theory. Monocausal explanations rarely explain anything. While the Great Man Theory helps explain the rise of Chinggis Khan and the early Mongol Empire, it does not necessarily explain the success of the Mongols after Chinggis Khan's death.

Undoubtedly, the military machine Chinggis Khan created assisted in the expansion of the Mongol Empire. Yet, while he initially organized the army as well as introducing new tactics, the military continued to evolve after his death. It is safe to say that the Mongol Empire could not have succeeded without the military. Numerous steppe empires existed prior to the Mongol, but none enjoyed the extent of conquests and the successes that the Mongol military did. While popularly conceived as a mob of horse-archers and sabre-wielding barbarians, the Mongol military was much more complex than this stereotype.[8]

As many empires have learned, however, it is much easier to conquer than to rule. The fact that the Mongols provided stable rule over most of their territories indicates that their governmental style also contributed to their success. In the past, it was thought that the Mongols largely left the actual running of the government to personnel they recruited from their conquered territories, particularly Uighurs, Khitans, and Persians who had a long history of running empires and kingdoms.[9] Recent scholarship, however, has demonstrated that this is not true and the Mongols took great interest in administration.[10] Indeed, one could argue that the empire was not just an empire but also a family business of the *altan urugh* or the Golden Kin (the family of Chinggis Khan). Furthermore, the Mongols created a dual system of military and civil administration consisting of Mongol and non-Mongol personnel and techniques. This apparatus, staffed through a system of meritocracy, provided them with the flexibility required to run a trans-continental empire.

While bureaucracies are able to run without a particular idea other than to sustain itself as well as the government which it serves, government ultimately implement policies in order to effect change or to guide it. The Mongols were no different. As their goal was to rule the world as indicated in their ideology, the Mongols also implemented policies to assist in that effort which included creating stability and order to their empire. Two policies in particular helped this aim. The first was the Mongols' policy of religious tolerance.

In an era in which religious driven warfare and discrimination was common, the Mongols' approach was startling to outsiders. Indeed, most had difficulty believing that the Mongols did not prefer one religion over another and most faiths tried to sway them to their particular belief system. The Mongols however remained neutral and favoured none. The second policy that contributed to their success was their promotion of commerce. As former American President Bill Clinton once famously said, "It's the economy, stupid." While the economy does not drive all aspects of a state, it plays an important role in any society. The Mongols instituted policies that assisted the expansion of trade not only within the Mongol Empire but ultimately had long lasting effects even after their demise. Due to their policies, some have given the Mongols credit for the first appearance of globalism. While it may be a stretch to apply a twenty-first century concept to a thirteenth-century empire, like all myths, there is some truth to it. The Mongol court's embracing of commerce helped fund their empire, yet it, along with their religious policy, also triggered other changes, which will be explored in detail later.

The factors listed above all contributed to the Mongol success, but to fully understand how the aspects of the empire contributed to the success of the Mongol Empire they must be examined separately. This examination is all the more important as all of the factors that contributed to their success also contributed to the demise of the empire. As with so many things, we must begin with the rise of Chinggis Khan.

Notes

[1] The dates for the early life of Chinggis Khan are approximate. It is generally agreed that his birth was in 1162, but this is by no means certain. Other possibilities are 1167 or 1155. Thus, the chronology must be adapted according to the birth. We know Temüjin was nine-years old when his father was poisoned.

[2] Larry W. Moses, "A Theoretical Approach to the Process of Inner Asian Confederation," *Études Mongoles* 5 (1974): 113–22.

[3] Michal Biran, *The Empire of the Qara Khitai in Eurasian History* (Cambridge: Cambridge University Press, 2005), 46.

[4] Neil Pederson, et al., "Pluvials, Droughts, the Mongol Empire, and Modern Mongolia," *Proceedings of the National Academy of Sciences* 111, no. 12 (March 2014), 4375–79.

[5] E. H. Carr, *What Is History?* (New York: Vintage, 1961), 67–69.

[6] Christopher R. Versen, "What's Wrong with a Little Social Darwinism (In Our Historiography)?," *The History Teacher* 42, no. 4 (2009), 406–8.

[7] Versen, "What's Wrong," 407.

[8] See Timothy May, *The Mongol Art of War* (Barnsley: Pen & Sword, 2007 & 2016).

[9] David Morgan, *The Mongols*, 2nd ed. (Malden: Blackwell, 2007), 94–98; David O. Morgan, "Who Ran the Mongol Empire?," *Journal of the Royal Asiatic Society* 1 (1982): 124–36.

[10] Morgan, *The Mongols*, 194; David O. Morgan, "Mongol or Persian: The Government of Ilkhanid Iran," *Harvard Middle Eastern and Islamic Review* 3 (1996): 62–76.

Chapter 1

The Rise of Chinggis Khan and the Mongol Empire

When Temüjin, the man who became Chinggis Khan, was born, the Mongols were but one of several groups vying to power. Shattered both militarily and politically by the Jin Empire and Tatars in the 1160s, the Mongols lacked a khan to unify them. Most of what we know of Chinggis Khan's early life comes from one of the few Mongol sources related to the Mongol Empire: *The Secret History of the Mongols*.[11] The general narrative that follows is taken from the *Secret History*.

Temüjin's Rise to Power

Temüjin's rise to power faced many obstacles. Yesügei, murdered when Temüjin was approximately nine years old, had proven to be a strong military leader although he was not a khan. With his death, most of Yesügei's *nökhöd* (sworn companions) abandoned his family and sought service with more promising leaders, including the rival Tayichi'ud clan. Hö'elün, Temüjin's mother attempted to hold the family together but also faced the challenge of raising her sons alone, a difficult task given a developing rivalry between Temüjin and his elder brother, Bekhter (the son of Yesügei's second wife). Despite their dire circumstances, lacking flocks of sheep and possessing few horses, Temüjin murdered Bekhter as the latter stole food from Temüjin and his brother Jochi Qasar

Temüjin also spent an indeterminate time as a captive and perhaps slave amongst the Tayichi'ud. This may have been for his crime of fratricide or perhaps simply as a method to reduce any prestige that Yesügei's family may have still held. He eventually escaped and began to restore the fortunes of his family. Shortly before his father's death, Temüjin had been betrothed to Börte, the daughter of Dei Sechen of the Onggirad who saw something promising in Temüjin. Dei Sechen told Yesügei,

> This son of yours is a boy
> Who has fire in his eyes,
> Who has light in his face.[12]

Dei Sechen was indeed correct about Temüjin, even if it took years before his auspicious nature became apparent to others. Now married, Temüjin then used her wedding dowry to secure the protection and patronage of Toghril, Khan of the powerful Kereit confederation in central Mongolia.

Although fortune now seemed to smile on Temüjin, it was fleeting. The Merkit tribe attacked him, seeking vengeance. Hö'elün had originally been the wife of a Merkit leader, but Yesügei kidnapped her as the two were returning to Merkit territory. While Temüjin and his brothers fled for their lives, the Merkit took Börte back to their camp. Months went by before Temüjin could rescue his now pregnant wife with the support of Toghril and Temüjin's *anda* or blood brother, Jamuqa. With victory, Temüjin gained valuable war experience under the tutelage of Jamuqa and stayed with his *anda* after their victory.

Börte gave birth to Jochi in Jamuqa's camp, where Temüjin renewed the bonds of friendship.[13] Jochi's birth was problematic as it was uncertain as to whether Temüjin or a Merkit was the child's father. Temüjin accepted the child as his own—bride kidnapping was, unfortunately, not uncommon on the medieval steppe. Jochi's birth, however, resurfaced later in the history of the Mongol Empire as a divisive force.

Eventually Temüjin parted ways from Jamuqa, relying heavily on the advice of his mother and wife. His time with Jamuqa was time well spent as Temüjin learned much about leadership—not only how to be successful, but also aspects to avoid, as evinced by the number of Jamuqa's followers who departed with Temüjin. These included not only high-ranking members of the Mongol elite, but also commoners who saw Temüjin as a different type of leader—someone who did not cling to a rigid social hierarchy, but valued individuals for their talents over their heritage. Others also viewed Temüjin as being special and more charismatic. One former supporter of Jamuqa left Temüjin as

> [...] a heavenly sign appeared before my very eyes, revealing the future to me. There came a fallow cow. She circled Jamuqa and struck his tent-cart with her horns; then she butted him breaking one of her horns.[...]Then a hornless and fallow ox lifted up the great shaft under the tent, harnessed it on to himself and pulled it after him. As he proceeded following Temüjin on the wide road, he kept bellowing, "Together Heaven and Earth have agreed: Temüjin shall be lord of the people!"[14]

While Jamuqa initially accepted Temüjin's departure, tensions quickly grew. A follower of Temüjin killed Jamuqa's relative Taichar after the latter rustled some horses. War quickly followed. Despite being relatively equal in strength, Jamuqa's experience won the day. Temüjin was soundly defeated and departed Mongolia. The sources are vague as to what exactly happened, other than hints that he was somewhere in the Jin Empire.[15]

In 1196, Temüjin returned to Mongolia. He quickly resumed his position over his former followers, in part because Jamuqa's wrath continued to alienate many Mongols; boiling people alive has that effect on people.[16] Jamuqa's victory over Temüjin had a ripple effect, leading to Toghril's overthrow. Temüjin was key in restoring Toghril to power and the two men forged a strong a bond between them and this increased Temüjin's status. Working together, they transformed the Kereit into one of the dominant powers on the steppes. Their success did not go unnoticed and a confederation formed against them, consisting of the Naiman, Tatars, Merkit, and Mongols. This rival confederacy was led by Jamuqa, who assumed the title of *Gur-Khan* (universal ruler) in 1201. Despite Jamuqa's use of weather-magic to summon a storm against Toghril and Temüjin, they emerged victorious. With the Gur-Khanid confederation shattered, Temüjin used the opportunity to take vengeance on the Tayichi'ud. He defeated them despite suffering a grievous throat wound in a battle by the Onan River in northern Mongolia.[17]

Temüjin continued his success in eastern Mongolia and finally ended his decades-long feud with the Tatars in 1202. He decided to eradicate the Tatars as a tribe. As tribal identity was based on the identity of the leading clans, Temüjin simply eliminated all of the Tatar male elite who were taller than the linchpin of an ox cart, thus leaving only women and young children.[18] The victory not only eliminated a powerful rival, but made Temüjin the most powerful figure in eastern Mongolia.

Temüjin's success did not go unnoticed in Toghril's camp. Here, the ageing khan found himself in a maelstrom of his own insecurity and the jealous conniving of Temüjin's rivals. Jamuqa, back in the service of Toghril, whispered against his *anda* while Senggüm, Toghril's son, worried that Temüjin might become the heir to his father's throne. Additionally, Mongol aristocrats openly complained to Toghril about Temüjin. Temüjin had made a habit of doling out more equitable shares of plunder, not basing them solely on lineage. While it strengthened the loyalty of the commoners, the aristocrats found their privileged position under threat. On top of this Temüjin audaciously proposed that his son Jochi marry Senggüm's daughter Cha'ur.[19]

The conspirators convinced Toghril that through the pretext of a wedding, they could lure Temüjin into a trap. They would have gotten away with it too, if not for some meddling herdsmen who overheard the plan. They informed Temüjin. While he escaped death, it did not prevent war in 1203. Although the Kereit were initially successful, Temüjin managed to regroup his forces and launch a counterattack, defeating the Kereit. Both Toghril and Senggüm escaped but by different routes. Toghril wandered into Naiman territory where he was killed when a scout failed to recognize him. Senggüm, however, fled into Xi Xia and temporarily found refuge.[20]

Temüjin did not execute the leadership of the Kereit; he knew many of them intimately from his years of service with Toghril. The Kereit were incorporated and the leadership connected to the Temüjin through marriage. Jaqa Gambu, Toghril's brother, still remained and could have potentially become a threat, but Temüjin neutralized him by marrying his daughter Ibaqa. Additionally, Tolui, Temüjin's youngest son married Ibaqa's sister, Sorqoqtani and Begtümish, another sister, married Jochi.

Thus, in two different manners Temüjin tied rival powers to him. The hostility between the Tatars and Mongols was too great to reconcile. By eliminating the leading clans of the Tatars and incorporating the commoners, Temüjin replaced the identity of the Tatars by providing a new one centred on him. He also married two Tatar sisters. As he had longstanding ties with the Kereit, the method was different. As evinced by the rumours swirling in Toghril's camp, there were clearly factions that did not oppose Temüjin's leadership. The marriages between Temüjin's family and that of Jaqa Gambu merged the Kereit in to the Mongols without further resistance. The Kereit leadership was replaced with Temüjin's family, but rather than complete removal, Jaqa Gambu's family became incorporated into it.

With the demise of Toghril and Temüjin only beginning to assert his authority in central Mongolia, a power vacuum emerged. The Naiman, the dominant group in western Mongolia saw an opportunity to seize the former Kereit pastures, particularly the important Orkhon river basin. As the Naiman began to gather their forces and seek out allies, Temüjin learned of their intent. Forewarned, Temüjin made a desperate march across Mongolia to attack the Naiman before they could fully gather their strength. The two armies met at Chakirma'ut in 1204. Despite the Naiman having a more advantageous position (the high ground), Temüjin proved more skilful in deploying his troops. By nightfall, the Naiman were pushed back to the Naqu Cliffs, with many being pushed off, their bodies stacking up like logs.[21]

Temüjin Enthroned as Chinggis Khan, 1206

Although some resistance remained, it was sparse. By 1206, Temüjin united the steppes. At a *quriltai* in 1206, he was formally enthroned as Chinggis Khan, meaning firm or resolute leader. At this *quriltai,* he began to organize a rudimentary government. He apportioned troops to his generals as well as to his family, designating regions for their pastures. He also restructured society to eliminate tribal identities. Rather than various tribes, they were all now part of the *Yeke Monggol Ulus* or Great Mongol State. His family became the Golden Kin or *Altan Urugh* and the only aristocracy within the realm. Groups loyal to him remained largely intact; those who had resisted him were divided up and distributed among the loyalists for incorporation into military units.

Additionally, he began to construct institutions to run his new realm. The most important was the *keshig* or bodyguard. Ten thousand men were recruited to form the *keshig*, greatly expanding it from the few hundred that served him in 1204. *Keshig* members (*keshigten*) included the sons of his commanders. In addition to serving as guards, the *keshigten* served as hostages, binding their families to Chinggis Khan. Only a few thousand guarded the khan on any day. The other members of the *keshig* also assumed household duties, such as tending Chinggis Khan's flocks and herds, cooking his food, and holding his cup. These seemingly tedious duties demonstrated the *keshigten's* versatility and provided Chinggis Khan with a household of individuals he could trust. As he learned their abilities, members were promoted to become generals or found service as governors while retaining their rank in the *keshig*. Thus, Chinggis Khan could position his loyal supporters through his realm and later empire, rather relying solely on family members who often had their own agendas and rivalries.

Chinggis Khan organized his new society along decimal lines (tens, hundreds, and thousands) and assigned commanders to the *minggans* (units of a thousand). While Chinggis Khan's family also received *minggans*, Chinggis Khan designated the unit commanders. Many of the new commanders rose from the rank of commoners, some having been Temüjin's earliest companions, to become some of the most important figures in the empire. This included Jelme and his relative, Sübedei who became the greatest general in the Mongol Empire. Defeated tribesmen were sprinkled among the regiments. Once assigned to a unit, they remained there. They could not transfer from their unit, thus Chinggis Khan prevented the defeated tribes from ever reforming. The sole exception to this were the Kereit as discussed above. In doing so, Chinggis Khan attempted to forge a single identity. All of the nomads were now Mongols and part of the *Yeke Monggol Ulus* or Great Mongol Nation.

Chinggis Khan began to consider other potential threats. Although Toghril was dead, Senggüm fled to Xi Xia. Additionally, Güchülüg, a Naiman prince escaped after Chakirma'ut. Another concern remained further south. Qara Khitai had longed held influence over the Naiman while the Jin often meddled in steppe affairs to prevent a single power from dominating the steppes. In the early twelfth century, the Jin ensured the fracturing of the first Mongol khanate, then in the 1190s, they enlisted Temüjin's and Toghril's aid to shatter the Tatars who had become a menace to the Jin borders. Would the Jin attempt to rally discontented tribes to break Chinggis Khan's nascent khanate? Would Qara Khitai attempt to assert their authority over the weakened Naiman? Certainly, these questions haunted Chinggis Khan's thoughts.

As it is often said, timing is everything. Other events prevented the states neighbouring the Mongolian steppes from immediately intervening in Mongolia. Entering the thirteenth century, Qara Khitai's dominance in Central Asia had imperceptibly weakened. Meanwhile, the Jin were preoccupied with rebellious *jüyin,* the various nomadic and sedentary groups that served as a frontier buffer. Neither state could interfere as Chinggis Khan consolidated his authority. Chinggis Khan took advantage of his good fortune.

Expansion Outside Mongolia under Chinggis Khan

It is at this point that the Mongols began to expand outside of Mongolia. As early as 1205, Mongol raiders invaded Xi Xia, allegedly in search of Senggüm who had found only temporary refuge in Xi Xia. He and his remaining forces made themselves unwelcome after indiscriminate pillaging. Other forces began to track other potential threats. In 1207, Jochi, Chinggis Khan's eldest (and perhaps illegitimate son), led an army northward against the *Hoi-yin Irgen* or Forest People—the various groups living in the forests of Siberia north of Mongolia. Ouduqa Beki, the leader of the Oirat, promptly submitted. He had been among the Gur-Khanid forces arrayed against Temüjin and Toghril in 1201, and then the Oirats came to the aid of the Naiman at Chakirma'ut. Resistance undoubtedly meant destruction.

To ensure Oirat loyalty, Chinggis Khan married his eldest daughter Chechiyegen to Ouduqa Beki's eldest son. Chechiyegen, served as her father's viceroy and the power behind the Oirat throne; this became a normal practice with the daughters of Chinggis Khan.[22] Ouduqa Beki served as an example and most of the *Hoi-yin Irgen* promptly surrendered with minimal resistance. The addition of these Siberian peoples allowed Chinggis Khan to isolate the Merkit, who abandoned their homelands. Indeed, a number submitted to Chinggis Khan and those that remained (led by Toqto'a Beki) joined the Naiman prince Güchülüg near the Irtysh River. The *Hoi-yin Irgen's* submission also secured his northern borders while providing access to the lucrative fur trade as well as grain and gold from the Yenisei River basin.

Chinggis Khan did not ignore the shadow cast by Güchülüg. In 1207, he led an army over the Altai Mountains in search of the Naiman and Merkit refugees. He found and defeated them at the Battle of the Irtysh River in 1208; the defeated Naiman and Merkit continued their retreat. Although Chinggis Khan withdrew, Sübedei continued the pursuit and defeated them again at the Chu River. From here, the Naiman first sought refuge among the Uighurs and then the Qarluqs, both of whom repulsed the Naiman, deeming them little more than bandits. Güchülüg, however, found refuge in Qara Khitai, where he converted from Nestorian Christianity to Buddhism and married the Gur Khan's daughter.[23] Meanwhile, the Merkit fled further west, finding refuge among the Qangli Turks.

As the Qangli refused to hand over the Merkit, the Mongols attacked and defeated both of them. On Sübedei's return towards Mongolia, he had a brief encounter with Muhammad Khwārazmshāh, the ruler of Khwārazm, who had his own axe to grind with the Qangli Turks. Although Sübedei attempted to avoid conflict, the Khwārazmians insisted on battle. Under the cover of night, the Mongols withdrew so that Muhammad found himself unopposed the following day. Nonetheless, the encounter affected him—despite possessing a numerical edge, his army proved no match for the Mongols. It was an encounter that haunted him for the next ten years.[24]

While Sübedei returned to Mongolia, he found that Chinggis Khan secured the western frontier by sending his son-in-law or *güregen,* Toquchar to the western frontier with a small army. Toquchar's presence also induced the Uighurs, perhaps perturbed that Güchülug was now the son-in-law of the Gur-Khan, to transfer their loyalty from Qara Khitai to Chinggis Khan. The Idiqut, or ruler of the Uighurs, personally submitted to Chinggis Khan. Chinggis Khan rewarded him by considering him his fifth son and married his daughter Al Altan to the Idiqut. The Qarluqs followed suit in 1211 after sighting Mongol units near the city of Almaliq.

Meanwhile, Chinggis Khan continued his raids into Xi Xia, which proved incapable of defeating Chinggis Khan's forces. While the raids yielded plentiful plunder, they also served the purpose of forging a new identity among the nomads of Mongolia. The *Yeke Monggol Ulus* truly came into being through these foreign adventures—the tribesmen lacked the time and energy to resume feuds that had wracked the steppes of Mongolia for the past four decades. Now they fought side by side against opponents who saw no difference between a Mongol, Merkit, or Naiman. They all looked the same and fought the same—to a peasant or merchant in Xi Xia, what was the difference? They all killed and plundered the same. In 1209, Xi Xia finally submitted after the Mongols nearly captured the Tangut capital through siege warfare. Although the Mongols had yet to master siege warfare, their efforts at flooding the city proved sufficiently threatening that the Tangut saw tribute as a more viable option than warfare. In addition to silk, silver, and gold, the Mongols received numerous camels as well as the princess Chaqa as a bride for Chinggis Khan. A marriage alliance now tied the Tangut and the Mongols together. With the matter resolved, Chinggis Khan withdrew his troops and refrained from occupying Xi Xia.[25]

His eyes now turned to the Jin Empire, who had finally suppressed the *jüyin* rebellion. A new emperor (Emperor Wei Shao Wang r. 1209–1213) sat on the throne, different from the one (Emperor Zhaozong r. 1190–1209) who sought Temüjin assistance against the Tatars. When Jin envoys met Chinggis Khan, they instructed that he show obeisance and send tribute to the new Altan Khan (the term used by the Mongols for the Jin Emperor). According to one source, Chinggis Khan spat at the emperor's name and rode away.[26] War had begun.

Mongol armies invaded in 1211. They raided and pillaged, defeating Jin armies when they encountered them. They did not seek to take Zhongdu, the Jin capital nor occupy territory. Instead, they solidified their control over the tribes south of the Gobi desert as well as occupy the mountain passes that led from the Jin Empire to Mongolia. Warfare continued until 1214, forcing the Jin to the offer peace terms. With that, the Mongols withdrew, laden with plunder and tribute.

Peace proved short-lived, however, as the new Jin Emperor, Xuanzong (r. 1213–1224) withdrew from Zhongdu to Kaifeng, further south, as Zhongdu proved vulnerable to the Mongols. Chinggis Khan viewed this as a violation of their peace treaty.[27] In his eyes, the Jin must be up to something, otherwise why would they move away from the capital? The Mongol armies returned intent on seizing Zhongdu, which fell to the Mongols in 1215. Nonetheless, the Jin continued to resist. Even as the Mongols regularly demolished the Jin field armies, they were forced to take cities one by one. Despite a rebellion among the *Hoi-yin Irgen*, the Mongols seemed certain to finish the conquest of the Jin, but other events interfered.

Mongol forces began to penetrate Qara Khitai in search of Güchülüg. Güchülüg, however, usurped the throne of his father-in-law, the Gur Khan Yelü Zhilugu in 1211. No longer restrained by respect for the Gur Khan and the Jin Empire now weakened, Chinggis Khan dispatched Jebe to hunt down Güchülüg. Hated by the population for Güchülüg's oppressive rule, the populace viewed the Mongols as liberators.[28] Güchülüg fled from region to region but found no succour and was killed in the environs of Afghanistan. Jebe paraded Güchülüg's head through Qara Khitai as evidence of the Mongol victory. With that, Qara Khitai became part of the Mongol Empire.

The Mongol Empire now bordered the Khwārazmian Empire. Muhammad II Khwārazmshāh had been a vassal of Qara Khitai, but joined Güchülüg in overthrowing the Gur Khan. They had agreed to split the empire between them. After the Gur Khan's defeat, however, the Naiman and Khwārazmshāh fought over Māwarānnahr, the region between the Syr Darya and Amu Darya rivers. With Güchülüg preoccupied by the Mongols, Muhammad II quickly gained control of the coveted region.

The Mongols sought trade with Khwārazm and sent a caravan to the border city of Otrār. The governor, Inalchuq, massacred the caravan on charges of espionage, perhaps on Muhammad's orders. The charges were not inaccurate, albeit the riches carried by the caravan must have also attracted Inalchuq's attention. Undoubtedly, there were spies among the caravaneers, but merchants, regardless of whom they served, carried intelligence and served as spies regardless of their intent. As they traversed the trade routes they undoubtedly knew local conditions in terms of security, commerce, as well as bits of news that when linked together provided a nice overview. Thus, even if the merchant was not directly serving as a spy, careful questioning could glean intelligence from a merchant or camel tender. Indeed, only a camel tender escaped the massacre and brought the news to Chinggis Khan.

The massacre in 1218 did not immediately lead to war. Chinggis Khan, preoccupied with the Jin Empire and just in the wake of the *Hoi-yin Irgen* rebellion, did not seek a war on his far western frontier. He sought to resolve the matter diplomatically, asking for the return of his goods, as the Mongol ruler and many of the elite had invested in the caravan. He also requested that the governor be turned over to him for punishment.

Muhammad Khwārazmshāh rejected the terms by killing the diplomat and burning the beards of the Mongol guards. He could not turn over Inalchuq as they were related, but the governor could have also implicated Muhammad's own complicity in the massacre. Additionally, Muhammad took offence to Chinggis Khan's message in which he referred to Muhammad Khwārazmshāh as his fifth son, thus conferring an inferior status to the Muslim ruler. Muhammad viewed himself as a second Alexander the Great. His empire stretched from the Syr Darya to the Indus River and almost to the Zagros Mountains in Iran. Indeed, Muhammad ruled the most powerful empire in the Islamic World.

The Khwārazmshāh's offences to his envoys enraged Chinggis Khan. Empowering the general Muqali as his viceroy, he tasked him with finishing the campaign against the Jin Empire and made his brother Temüge regent in Mongolia, while Chinggis Khan led an army from Mongolia to Khwārazm. Even with Mongol outposts in Qara Khitai, it took months before the Mongols could invade. Muhammad had his own intelligence network; thus the Mongol invasion did not take him by surprise. In the lull before war, Muhammad improved his fortifications and stationed his troops at strongholds across Māwarānnahr—as a recently acquired region, he could not depend on it remaining loyal without a strong military presence.

The onslaught came swiftly and the Mongols quickly captured Otrār.[29] Inalchuq resisted bravely, but was captured and executed by pouring molten silver down his throat. From Otrār, the Mongol armies divided and struck at multiple points. The army led by Chinggis Khan, however, disappeared into the Kyzyl Kum desert, rumoured to be impenetrable. He appeared weeks later, three hundred miles behind enemy lines at Bukhara, where the goods from the Otrār caravan were allegedly stored. The city fell quickly and the city elders submitted to Chinggis Khan. He then ascended the *minbar* or pulpit in the Friday Mosque, the largest mosque in this venerable city. From there he harangued the population, saying:

> O people, know that you have committed great sins, and that the great ones among you have committed these sins. If you ask me what proof I have for these words, I say it is because I am the punishment of God. If you had not committed great sins, God would not have sent a punishment like me upon you.[30]

Chinggis Khan questioned them as to the whereabouts of his possessions—the loot from his massacred caravan and the true reason for the invasion. The city was systematically searched and plundered. The population was then divided into those who were massacred, those who became arrow fodder, and those who had skills the Mongols valued such as craftsmen. Many would return with the Mongols to Mongolia.

While fast-moving armies led by his sons continued to reduce other cities, Chinggis Khan led his army against Samarqand, the capital of Māwarānnahr. In the face of certain defeat, Muhammad Khwārazmshāh crossed the Amu Darya and fled into Khurāsān. Chinggis Khan dispatched Jebe and Sübedei in pursuit. They chased him across Iran until Muhammad finally fled to an island in the Caspian Sea where he died of dysentery. The pursuit of Muhammad Khwārazmshāh prevented the Khwārazmians from organizing a coherent resistance.

One of Muhammad's sons, Jalāl al-Dīn, however was able to rally support in what is now Afghanistan. He successfully defeated a Mongol army near Kabul. This, however, attracted Chinggis Khan's attention and he personally led an army against the prince, whom he defeated at the Indus River. Meanwhile, Chinggis Khan's youngest son, Tolui ravaged Khurāsān. Cities that submitted promptly were spared; those that resisted or rebelled were obliterated. One observer wrote that the region would not recover for a thousand years.[31]

While this proved to be hyperbole, it did speak to the level of destruction and fear that the Mongols promoted.

The Mongols withdrew in 1223 upon receiving word that Xi Xia rebelled that year. While the Mongol army withdrew from the region, they occupied only up to the Amu Darya, leaving modern Afghanistan and much of Iran destroyed. Jebe and Sübedei, however, did not immediately join Chinggis Khan; they had permission to explore the western regions after Muhammad Khwārazmshāh's death.

With that, the generals ventured into Transcaucasia and ravaged Armenia and Georgia before crossing the Caucasus Mountains. Jebe and Sübedei then crossed these mountains where they defeated the Kipchaks and other nomads. While the Mongols had no desire to engage the Rus', marriage alliances between Kipchak khans and Rus' princes made it inevitable. The combined army proved to be no match for the Mongols, who lured them deep into the Pontic Steppes. Although the Mongols defeated them at the Battle of the Kalka River in 1223, the Mongols did suffer a loss as Jebe was struck down during the initial stages of the battle.[32] Sübedei then withdrew into the Caspian steppes to rendezvous with the armies of Jochi.

Meanwhile, Chinggis Khan had returned to Mongolia where he rested his army. He tried to resolve the Xi Xia rebellion diplomatically. This came to naught. The Mongols began the invasion of Xi Xia in March 1226. Once again, the Tangut learned that they could not stand against the Mongols in the field. They also learned to their detriment that the Mongols no longer attempted clumsy sieges. Instead, their war machines systematically reduced the Tangut fortresses one by one. During this time of methodical warfare, Chinggis Khan chose to go hunting. Startled by a herd of *qulan* or wild asses, Chinggis Khan's horse threw him. While the fall did not cause immediate death, he suffered internal injuries and was bed-ridden for the final siege. While his generals insisted that he end the siege of the Tangut capital, Zhongxing, Chinggis Khan refused saying "While I take my meals you must talk about the killing and destruction of the Tang'ut and say,

'Maimed and tamed, they are no more'."[33] He also ordered his generals not to reveal his death until after the fall of the city.[34] True to their loyalty, his generals and sons executed his last wish. The city fell and the population massacred. Xi Xia disappeared from the map as the Mongols formally annexed it.

Ögodei, Successor to Chinggis Khan, and Further Expansion, 1229–1241

It took two years before the Mongols chose a new ruler. Part of the delay was that Chinggis Khan died outside of Mongolia and thus it took time to bury him. Indeed, even today no one knows where he is buried—in the Ordos region in Inner Mongolia in modern China, or perhaps the body was carried as far the Onan-Kerülen region in Mongolia, his ancestral home. Regardless, he had decreed that his third son Ögödei would be his successor. While an orderly succession was not guaranteed, his sons and generals remained faithful to Chinggis Khan's words and deeds and enthroned Ögödei.

The Mongols wasted little time resuming the conquests, now fuelled by an ideology that *Köke Möngke Tengri*, the Blue Eternal Heaven, had bequeathed the earth to Chinggis Khan and his descendants to rule. Thus, anyone who did not submit to them rebelled against the will of Heaven. Their justification of their claim was simple: if it was not true, then how could one explain the conquests of Chinggis Khan?

In 1230, Ögödei dispatched an army led by Chormaqan to the Middle East as Jalal al-Din had resurfaced and sought to restore the Khwārazmian Empire. One portion stymied those attempts as the Mongols occupied Khurāsān and brought the regions of Ghazna and Ghūr in modern Afghanistan under Mongol control. Meanwhile, Chormaqan Noyan led the main army into Iran, subduing most of northern Iran. The rulers of the principalities in southern Iran offered their submission before Mongol armies marched in their direction. Their defection from Jalāl al-Dīn's cause is surprising until one realizes that while Jalāl al-Dīn proved to be an exceptional warrior, he was a lousy ruler. Indeed, some rulers considered him a nuisance on par, if not greater than, with the Mongols.[35] Many were relieved when the adventurer died under somewhat mysterious circumstances in 1231.[36] After stabilizing the region, the Mongols then turned their attention to Transcaucasia and brought Armenia and Georgia under Mongol control in by 1239.

Meanwhile, the main Mongol armies renewed the war against the Jin Empire. With Muqali's death in 1223, the Jin had regained some territory. A new Mongol offensive led by Tolui and Sübedei reversed the tables. While Chinggis Khan was unable to finish off the Jin Empire, Ögödei's almost single-minded attention to it allowed the Mongols to focus the majority of their military activities to progressively reducing the Jin Empire, even though Tolui died in 1232. The hammer fell with the capture of Kaifeng in 1233. The Jin Emperor escaped to Caizhou, but by then the Jin's destruction was a forgone conclusion with final destruction occurring in early 1234.

Events were not settled in China despite the Mongol victory. In the later stages of the Jin war, the Mongols formed an alliance with the Song Empire (960–1127), who saw an opportunity to regain territory lost to the Jin. The Song contributed little in terms of military aid. Indeed, while the Jin usually lost to the Mongols on the battlefield, they still proved superior to the Song. The Song, however, did provide much needed logistical aid in terms of food supplies. Almost immediately after the war's conclusion, however, the Song crossed swords with the Mongols in an attempt to claim territory. Although Ögödei had given the Jin all of his attention, he viewed this a border conflict and devoted fewer resources to it.

Mongol Expansion Westward, 1236–1242

Ögödei's true attention was on the Western Campaign. Ögödei assembled a combined army of the Mongol princes to assist the Jochids in carving out their patrimony. Although Jochi died in 1225, he left numerous sons including Batu, Orda, and Berke. Although Orda was the eldest, Batu became the leader of the house of Jochi. With Batu as the nominal leader and

Sübedei as the operational commander, the Mongols set out towards the Volga River in 1236. The great city of Bulgar fell and the Mongols brought the Kipchaks in the Caspian steppes to heel; these Kipchaks were then incorporated into the Mongol army, although some escaped and fled west.

While Mongol forces continued to strike against the Kipchaks, in the winter of 1237, the Mongols initiated operations against the Rus' princes. Although Russians winters have proven to be a formidable defence against invaders, the Mongols found it very much to their liking. The many rivers proved to be no trouble as they crossed the frozen water. Operating over hundreds of miles the Mongols subdued the northern Rus' cities quickly. Novgorod escaped destruction due to an early thaw, but it offered submission before the Mongols had an opportunity to reconsider.

In 1239, the Mongols completed their conquest of the Pontic and Kuban steppes, up to the Caucasus Mountains. Sübedei's operations there coincided with Chormaqan's conquest of Georgia. Thus, the Alans, Kipchaks, and others in the region had nowhere to flee. While the mountainous region gave haven to resistance, it was localized and never threatened Mongol control of the region.

The Mongols then turned their attention to Kiev. Although no longer the political capital of the Rus', it remained the religious and cultural centre. Despite the destruction wrought by the Mongols to the north, Kiev chose to resist. The city's leaders chose poorly. Not only did the ruling prince, Daniil flee, but the Mongols quickly penetrated the walls. While citizens attempted to take refuge in the many cathedrals, the Mongols simply set them on fire rather than attempt to storm them.

Not all sought the shelter of sanctuary. Others fled for their lives. Many Kipchaks lightened their load by selling their children to Italian slave dealers in the Crimea. These eventually found their way to the slave markets of the Middle East. Others continued to flee west. Forty thousand Kipchaks found refuge in Hungary.

The Mongols' invasion of Central Europe began in 1240. The Mongols demanded the return of the Kipchak refugees in Hungary, informing King Bela IV of Hungary that they were their slaves. Whether this was simply a construed *casus belli* or not matters little, Bela IV could not return them even if he desired (he did not). The Kipchaks ran afoul with his nobles and subjects who hanged Köten Khan, the Kipchak leader. The rest of the Kipchaks then fled south, rampaging through Hungary to make their escape. Regardless, the Mongols invaded Hungary while a smaller army invaded Poland. In both places, the Mongols pillaged and plundered as the Europeans marshalled their forces. In April of 1241, the Mongols won two brilliant victories. In Poland, Orda and Baidar defeated a combined army of Teutonic Knights, Polish nobility, and German miners at Liegnitz. Meanwhile, in Hungary, Sübedei and Batu crushed King Bela IV's army at the plain of Mohi near the Sajo River. King Bela survived Mohi but found little rest. He escaped only by fleeing to an island with the Mongols on his heels.

Despite panic spreading across Europe like the waves of the ocean, help was not forthcoming. Both Pope Gregory IX (r. 1227–1241) and the Holy Roman Emperor, Frederick II (r. 1220–1250) called for a crusade against the infidels, but little aid materialized as they vied against each other. Soon accusations arose that Frederick actually invited the Mongols to invade or that the Mongols were in league with the Jews as they were really the Ten Lost Tribes of Israel.[37] Duke Frederick of Austria was one of the few individuals to promise aid to Bela, but only after taking him captive and ransoming him for three provinces. Then Duke Frederick did nothing. The Mongols, surprisingly, withdrew across the Carpathians in 1242.

Many factors were involved in this withdrawal and scholars still debate the cause, but one of the underlying factors must have been the death of Ögödei. Ögödei probably drank himself to death, although there were some rumours that he was poisoned.[38] Regardless, a *quriltai* was needed. Chaghadai, now the senior prince, approved Ögödei's wives, Möge and Töregene as regents. Möge died not long afterwards, as did Chaghadai. Although the civil government of the Mongol Empire greatly improved during the era of Ögödei, Töregene replaced many of the ministers—many fled to safe havens rather than be arrested. Her administrative changes produced little outcry from the Mongol princes as she secured their support with lavish gifts—provided by the increased taxes and tribute brought about by her reforms.

Ögödei's Succession by Regents and Güyük, 1241–1251

Töregene did not organize a *quriltai* to select a new ruler until 1246. As she had secured the support of most of the princes over the past four years, her eldest son Güyük ascended the throne. It was not without challenge. Ögödei's grandson Shiremün was his chosen heir. Temüge, the youngest brother of Chinggis Khan also sought the throne and even toyed with the idea of a coup. He stayed his attempt at the last moment however. His claim was not without merit, as lateral successions between brothers was not uncommon among steppe empires.

Güyük did not forget Temüge's efforts however, although for the first few months of his reign, Töregene still held the reins of power. It appears that only after she died did Güyük actually assert his own authority. He then reversed many of her reforms, restoring the former ministers of state to power, at least those who survived her regency. Güyük also arrested and executed Temüge for his attempted coup, effectively ending any claim to the throne from outside of Chinggis Khan's descendants. He also renewed the Mongol conquests, which had gone dormant during the interregnum, with a few exceptions along the frontiers. While the Song front remained a stalemate, the Mongols conquered the Sultanate of Rum in 1243 and Trebizond, giving the Mongols most of modern Turkey.

To this end, Güyük sent reinforcements to the Song front as well as the Middle East. Güyük resolved to conquer Europe and gathered a new army. Sorqoqtani, the widow of Tolui warned Batu that Güyük's invasion was simply a cover to arrest Batu.[39] Güyük had disparaged him during the Western Campaign. As a result, Güyük had been sent to a livid Ögödei; and as a result, Güyük had not participated in the invasion of Central Europe. There is some doubt regarding this, but Batu had not attended Güyük's coronation, blaming his gout, and thus had not formally sworn allegiance.[40] As Güyük had to pass through Jochid territory to invade Europe, and would also require Jochid troops, Batu would have no option but to submit or fight Güyük, which did not seem prudent as his brothers, Berke and Orda, had sworn allegiance to the new *khaghan*.

Fate interceded, sparing both Europe from an invasion and possibly the Mongol Empire from a civil war. Güyük died en route and before crossing the Volga River. Whereas Batu avoided the political affairs of the empire immediately after Ögödei's death, Batu directed them following Güyük's death. He confirmed Oghul Qaimish, Güyük's widow, as the regent along with her sons, Naqu and Khwaja, stating that she should rule in consultation with the ministers. While Oghul Qaimish did not replace the ministers, she did not consult with them either. As such, she and her sons (who acted as rivals), issued their own, often conflicting, decrees or *jarliqs*. The empire unravelled as the central government's efficiency failed and princes began to follow their own whims, including on matters of taxation and governance.

Meanwhile, Batu held his own *quriltai* not in Mongolia, as was tradition, but in Jochid territory at Ala Qamaq, thought to be somewhere in modern Kazakhstan. Batu justified his decision once again on his chronic gout, which made the long journey to Mongolia impossible. At this *quriltai,* Batu conspired with Sorqoqtani to elect her eldest son, Möngke, to the throne. Möngke had served alongside Batu during the Western Campaign and proven his worth. The *quriltai*, however, was poorly attended although some Chaghatayids and Ögödeids attended, including Naqu and Khwaja. Oghul Qaimish's sons, though, did not stay for long. They both assumed that one or the other would be selected so they returned to their camps, leaving a proxy to vote with the majority, as they sought to avoid conflict with each other.

To their surprise, Möngke was selected and, to their chagrin, their proxy voted for Möngke as well, although he merely heeded Naqu and Khwaja's instructions. Möngke's enthronement, however, did not occur at the initial *quriltai* as it could only occur in Mongolia, at the traditional location in the Mongolian homeland by the Onan and Kerulen Rivers, which coincidentally was part of the Toluid *ulus* or patrimony. Again, Batu did not attend due to illness, but his brother Berke represented the Jochid interests and brought thirty thousand men to provide security for the enthronement. It proved a prudent decision.

Naqu grudgingly went but encountered an embittered Shiremün along the way. The two then conspired to assassinate Möngke and seize the throne. In their minds, the throne always belonged to the Ögödeids; who sat on the throne could be determined after the interlopers were put back in their place. They also counted on Chaghatayid support. Unfortunately, a stray camel foiled their plans.

The camel had strayed from the *quriltai.* One of Möngke's retainers, a falconer, stumbled upon Shiremün and Naqu's caravan while searching for it. As the animal would be marked with Möngke's *tamgha* or seal (in this case a brand), it would be easy enough to locate. Instead, he discovered the plot while assisting in repairing a broken wagon wheel. Innocently peeking into a wagon, he saw the armed soldiers, and deduced that the other wagons possessed similar contents. Kishik the falconer extricated himself from the conspirators and reported this to a disbelieving Möngke. Möngke finally dispatched his servitor, Menggeser, along with a sizeable force. Menggeser encountered the conspirators' camp. In no uncertain terms he made it clear that he would escort the princes to the *quriltai* and his men would ensure their wagons and supporters also made it safely to the camp. Naqu and Shiremun complied; to resist meant certain destruction.

Only after Möngke's enthronement did an investigation take place. Found guilty, both Naqu and Shiremün were sentenced to exile on the Song front. Many of their men were executed. A purge quickly followed with anyone connected to the conspirators being deemed complicit. This included not only immediate followers, but even old government hands such as Chinqai, who served as a minister under Chinggis Khan, Ögödei, as well as Güyük. Oghul Qaimish did not escape the purge either. After an investigation, where she remained defiant until the end while publicly mocking Möngke's legitimacy, the tribunal ordered her to be wrapped in felt and then drowned in a lake in Mongolia.

The Reign of Möngke, 1251–1259

While the purge was occurring, Möngke also instituted reforms to undo the damage caused during the interregnum. Censuses were conducted and he instituted strong central authority. With the reduction of the Ögödeids and many Chaghatayids, Möngke reallocated their territory. Much of the Ögödeid patrimony or *ulus* disappeared, swallowed by the Jochids and Toluids. Möngke also reformed the tax structure to restore a more rational and manageable system, as well as preventing Chinggisid princes from duplicating taxes. Conducting censuses throughout the empire, Möngke's government had a better understanding of the empire's resources. As a result, he lowered many taxes from the interregnum period, but imposed new ones that increased the government's revenue. A major reform also went to the *jam* or *yam* system, the pony-express style postal system that tied the empire together.

Möngke recalled all of the old *gerege* or *paizas* (passports) and issued new ones. During Oghul Qaimish's regency, the *jam* had come under duress as traffic increased. As Oghul Qaimish employed many merchants with ties to Chinggisid princes, or *ortoqs*, they mixed government business with commercial interests. As the *jam* stations fed and often replaced mounts for government messengers and officials, this became burdensome. Replacing a horse for a single messenger was normal, but many of these officials also wanted new camels for their baggage and they rode with a sizeable entourage. Further complicating matters was that the number of *gereges* had proliferated. Additionally, other Chinggisids had created their own *gerege* for their own territories, which overlapped with the imperial system and added more burdens to the nomads and villages that supplied the stations.[41] Faced with crippling demands, the nomads often migrated away from the stations and villagers abandoned their homes and fields rather than try to support a system that not only became burdensome, but broken.

Möngke then turned his attention to military matters. During his coronation, he undoubtedly noticed which local dynasts attended and which did not. Furthermore, he was well aware which foreign states had not submitted. In the Middle East, the Nizārī Ismāʿīlis remained outside the Mongols' dominion. Additionally, while the Abbasid Caliph in Baghdad and a number of Syrian potentates sent tribute, they had not actually tendered their obeisance in person. To bring these realms under proper Mongol authority, he dispatched his younger brother Hülegü with an army, reportedly a hundred and fifty thousand men comprised from units from throughout the empire.

Hülegü's march to Iran was leisurely. While part of it was due to the very nature of marching with a large army, it also allowed time for the preparation of pastures and provisions along the route, demonstrating the logistical capacity of the empire.[42] Undoubtedly, Hülegü's progress through former Ögödeid lands were meant to cow those princes as well as the Chaghatayids. After his coup, Möngke had appointed his own Chaghatayid khan, Qara Hülegü; he, however, died while returning to Central Asia. Thus his wife, Ergene Khatun, served as regent for Qara Hülegü's son, Mubārak Shāh. Hülegü's long stay at her court not only allowed disparate units from the various members of the *altan urugh* to join his army, but also reinforced the legitimacy of her reign.

While Hülegü made his way to Iran, other Mongol forces in the region campaigned against the Nizārīs. Mongol forces in Iran subdued much of the Nizārī territory by the time Hülegü arrived. Eventually, Khwurshāh, the Nizārī Imam or leader, submitted to the Mongols. They used him to secure the surrender of a number of fortresses in the mountainous regions south of the Caspian Sea. Some fortresses held out, but the Mongols took them one by one. In 1256, the great fortress of Alamūt, the Nizārī headquarters fell to a Mongol siege. Although a few fortresses continued to resist, the Mongols isolated them and eliminated the Nizārī threat.

Hülegü then marched towards Baghdad. While he attempted to secure the Caliph's submission by diplomatic means, it was hopeless. Part of the problem was the hubris of the Caliph who imagined his titular authority as the leader of the Sunni Muslim world bequeathed him with real power. The Abbasid Caliphate (750–1258) was by now a shadow of its halcyon era. As the Caliph claimed to be God's representative, there could be no room for such a figure in the Mongol Empire, whose legitimacy based itself on the idea that *Köke Möngke Tengri* or the Blue Eternal Heaven had given the earth to Chinggis Khan and his descendants. Only one such figure could exist, and that was Möngke.

Abbasid weakness in the face of the Mongols became apparent when Hülegü arrived. Hülegü's army consisted not only of the Mongols, but also Christian Armenians and Georgians. More notable, however, were the Muslims troops from Mosul, Shiraz, Kirman, and other kingdoms in Iran. Rather than swarming to defend the Caliphate, the Muslim dynasts within the Mongol Empire heeded their tributary agreements and provided troops as requested. Although Baghdad retained a regional significance after the Mongol sack, it never regained its international importance.

From there, Hülegü moved west, basing his army in the Mughan Steppe in Azerbaijan. His forces soon marched against the various cities in northern Iraq and Syria that had yet to submit. Many rulers quickly came to Hülegü and offered their submission. Those who failed to do so felt the wrath of the Mongols. Aleppo was one such city. Although Byzantine and Crusading armies had attacked it in the past, it never fell. The Mongols captured it in five days in early 1260. While Hülegü withdrew most of his army from Syria due to a shortage of pasture, Ked Buqa continued to reduce Sultan al-Nāṣir

Yūsuf's kingdom by capturing Damascus and then the sultan himself when he attempted to flee to Egypt.

Mongol occupation was short-lived. While their forces rested and consolidated Mongol control in Syria, the Mamluks of Egypt invaded. The Mamluks, former slave soldiers who had seized power in Egypt during the resultant chaos of the Seventh Crusade in 1250, decided to take the battle to the Mongols before the Mongols could invade. The two armies met at 'Ayn Jālūt in modern Israel. In a hard-fought battle, the Mamluks emerged victorious. The battle was a minor setback to the Mongols, at least at the time. They had been defeated before, but they always won the war. Events in the east, however, transformed the minor loss into a major victory for the Mamluks.

As the Song remained recalcitrant to Mongol rule, Möngke begun to give his southern neighbour his complete attention. The campaign began in 1252 with Möngke ordering his brother Qubilai to invade Dali, a kingdom on the southwestern border of China, the present-day Yunnan province in China, which would also open another front against the Song. Qubilai is said to have delayed his invasion due to illness but the veracity of this is suspect. While he may have suffered from gout (as he certainly did in his later years), Möngke suspected otherwise. Eventually, Qubilai sent his army ahead, led by Uriyangqadai, the son of Sübedei. While Uriyangqadai conquered the state, resistance continued until 1256. Now with more routes open and Möngke rule now secure, four Mongol armies entered the Song Empire in 1258, led by Möngke, Qubilai, Uriyangqadai, and "a grandson of one of Chinggis Khan's brothers."[43]

Although the inhospitable terrain of high mountains, humid rice paddies, and wide rivers stymied their advance, the Mongols slowly made headway against the Song Empire through sheer determination, pushing their way towards the Yangzi River. Unfortunately, Möngke died during this crucial push in 1259. News of his death brought the campaign to a halt. His son Asutai escorted the body back to Mongolia. While Möngke's third brother, Ariq Böke, began to arrange for a *quriltai* to select a new leader, while serving as Möngke's regent—a curious shift from the practice of wives serving as regent—Qubilai continued the campaign, determined to cross the Yangzi river and complete the conquest.[44]

Ariq Böke and Qubilai as Rival Khans, 1260–1264

Ariq Böke requested Qubilai to return to Mongolia and attend the *quriltai*, but Qubilai ignored the summons and continued his campaign. Only after he received word that his brother was proceeding with the *quriltai* did Qubilai halt his campaign. He then held his own *quriltai*, where he was chosen as the new *khaghan* in the spring of 1260. Ariq Böke was selected at the *quriltai* in Mongolia. Thus less than a year after Möngke's death the Mongol Empire now had two rivals to the throne who chose not to settle matters in the normal manner, at the *quriltai*, but in rival camps.

Although the brothers attempted to resolve the matter diplomatically, war soon began. Qubilai was the usurper in this war. He had chosen not to attend the *quriltai*. His efforts to cross the Yangzi and finish off the Song Empire look like a desperate ploy to gain the military credentials he lacked. Ariq Böke does not appear to have had much military experience on his résumé either, but he had served as Möngke's regent while Möngke invaded the Song Empire. What is curious is that none of Möngke's sons seems to have been considered for the throne.

Albeit the usurper, Qubilai drove Ariq Böke from Qaraqorum in 1262. As Qubilai controlled most of the armies in China (both Mongol and Han Chinese), he was able to cut off the supplies to the city, which required hundreds of cartloads of food every day.[45] Ariq Böke retreated to the Yenisei River basin, which provided him with grain as well as adequate pastures. The war now shifted to Central Asia. Ariq Böke sent Alghu, a Chaghatayid, to take control of the Chaghatayid Ulus (still ruled by the regent Ergene Khatun). Ariq Böke's reasoning was that the former Ögödeid and Chaghatayid domains would not only provide him with men and supplies, but would also open a second front. His plan backfired as Alghu betrayed him and sought to carve out his own independent realm. It is difficult to determine exactly when Alghu changed his mind, but Ergene Khatun's complaints about him certainly did not endear Alghu to Ariq Böke, as she was Ariq Böke's sister-in-law. Ariq Böke's position further worsened when Qubilai provided Alghu support. Unable to inflict a decisive defeat on Alghu, Ariq Böke's position grew weaker. In 1264, he submitted to Qubilai and died in prison in 1266. The war was over, but the empire was now splintered.

While Ariq Böke and Qubilai had been fighting, war also started between the Jochids and Hülegü. The primary point of conflict was over the status of Azerbaijan. The Jochids viewed it as part of their domain. The evidence suggests that at least during the reign of Möngke, Azerbaijan was indeed Jochid territory, and perhaps even parts of Iran.[46] This was not the case during Güyük's reign and thus must be viewed as a reward for Batu's aid in Möngke's enthronement. Hülegü's presence altered this. It should be remembered that Hülegü's campaign did not begin until after Batu's death. When it began, Berke was the Jochid Khan and one must wonder if Möngke had some misgivings, particularly after the two very brief reigns of Batu's son Sartaq and Ulaghchi, Sartaq's son, as well as perhaps a realization that the Jochids now controlled half of the empire. It is possible that Möngke never intended for Hülegü to remain in Azerbaijan and Iran, but expected him to carve out a new region perhaps in the Levant and Egypt.[47] Nonetheless, at the time of Möngke's death, Hülegü's conquests were at an impasse. His armies halted as he waited to see the results of the *quriltai.* At the same time, he had a falling out with the Jochid commanders in his forces. A few were executed on grounds of sorcery, to which Berke had no objections.[48] Others, however, fled to Jochid territory and Afghanistan, which was part of the Mongol Empire but not directly controlled by any Chinggisid prince as it was under *tamma* control and thus reported directly to the Khan. With no clear ruler, it was somewhat independent. Over the decades, control over much of Afghanistan swung between the Chaghatayid Khanate and then the Ilkhanate, as scholars have dubbed Hülegü's empire.

War between the Jochids and Hülegü started in late 1261. Hülegü defeated the Jochid forces in the Caucasus region. His situation became more dangerous as Berke formed an alliance with the Mamluks. As a Muslim, Berke found common cause with the Mamluks against Hülegü, who did not adhere to any particular religion, although he tended to favour Buddhists and Christians. While the two fought, events in Central Asia began to boil. Alghu continued to expand his realm at the expense of the remaining Ögödeids. It seemed as if he would complete the integration of the Ögödeid realm, but then in the mid-1260s, events took a different turn for the Mongol Empire.

Qubilai Khan Conquers the Song Dynasty but Is Defeated in Japan, 1265–1281

Ariq Böke's death in 1265 was followed by a series of deaths among the leading Mongols. Not only did Hülegü die in 1265, but Berke died the following year, unable to take advantage of his rival's death. Alghu also died in that year. The death of so many of the principal actors in the Mongol Empire created new opportunities. It permitted Qubilai to consolidate his control in Mongolia as well as Mongol domains in East Asia. Ergene attempted to have her son Mubārak Shāh enthroned. Qubilai objected, alleging that as the *khaghan* it needed his approval. He sent his own man, Baraq, a Chaghatayid who had served with Qubilai in China (most likely because of the Toluid Revolution). Baraq found sufficient support and became the khan. He then resumed the work of Alghu, but found that the situation had changed.

The leading Ögodeid prince, Qaidu, meanwhile was gaining support among the Jochids who became involved after Baraq had nibbled at their borders. With Jochid military aid from Möngke Temür, Berke's successor, Qaidu forced Baraq to the negotiation table at the Treaty of Qatwan in 1267. Here, the Jochids regained lost territory, as did Qaidu. In addition, Qaidu and Baraq split much of Māwarānnahr between them. Baraq was to be compensated with territory in Khurāsān, but he had to conquer it from the Ilkhans. Möngke Temür's real motivation appears here—to open another front against the Ilkhans. Abaqa, Hülegü's son and the new Ilkhan, however, decisively defeated Baraq at the Battle of Herat in 1270. Baraq fled back to his domains, but found himself betrayed as the majority of his army deserted to Qaidu. With Baraq's subsequent death, Qaidu took control of the Ögödeid and Chaghatayid *uluses*, placing Du'a on the Chaghatayid throne.

Despite dependence on Jochid aid, Qaidu proved to be nobody's puppet. The Jochids became increasingly leery of him, and even proposed an alliance between the Jochid *Ulus*, Ilkhanate and the Yuan (Qubilai's dynasty) against Qaidu.[49] Although Qaidu never claimed to be the *khaghan*, he also never recognized Qubilai as such. Qaidu was never a threat to take over East Asia, but he threatened Qaraqorum and the western frontiers of Qubilai's realm on numerous occasions. The border shifted frequently.

Qaidu's machinations did not prevent Qubilai from conquering the Song Empire however. The key element proved to be Qubilai's ties to the Ilkhans. From Abaqa he received two gifts. The first were Muslim engineers who built counterweight trebuchets, previously unknown in China. These allowed his armies to smash the strategic cities of Xiangyang and Fancheng. Secondly, he received the general Bayan. While Bayan's career with the Ilkhans was undistinguished, in China he proved to have exceptional genius and learned how to meld the Mongol cavalry with Chinese infantry and naval forces, the latter crucial on the wide rivers and coast of southern China. By 1279, the Song were defeated.

The victory over the Song did not give Qubilai the legitimation he had hoped for. The empire remained fragmented. His victory was significant, nonetheless. The war against the Song had began in 1234 and been prosecuted by four different khans: Ögödei, Güyük, Möngke, and Qubilai. Qubilai had the greatest success. Part of this was due to an attack on

Japan in 1274. The Mongol invasion at Hakata Bay was not an attempt to conquer Japan (although Qubilai probably would not have objected to that), but rather intended to destroy Hakata, the major trading point between the Song and Japan. By destroying Song trade, he weakened their economy, which had been so important in sustaining Song resistance to the Mongols.[50]

With the Song defeat, Qubilai intended to return to Japan and bring it in to the Mongol orbit. Fuelled not only by the Mongol ideology that the Mongols should rule the world, with the conquest of the Song Empire, Qubilai brought in another ideology, that of China as the Middle Kingdom. In this ideology, China was the centre of the world and neighbouring nations were part of a tribute system that recognized China's inherent cultural and civilizational superiority. This had broken down during the Song–Mongol war. He intended to restore it.[51] Korea finally submitted after numerous invasions. Mongol operations commenced against Japan, Pagan (Burma or Myanmar), Dai Viet and Champa (both comprise modern Vietnam). While Mongol armies were unable to conquer Southeast Asia, they did restore the tribute system—the rulers deemed it wiser to pay tribute than risk continued military action. Japan, however, proved to be a tougher nut to crack.

The Japanese eventually executed the envoys that Qubilai sent. He responded in 1281 by assembling the largest fleet in history until D-Day in 1944. This returns us to the Dark and Stormy night. The Japanese had learned from their previous encounters with the Mongols and denied them access to the beaches at Hakata. Another Mongol army (primarily Chinese) landed at another point and penetrated inland, but the battles became stalemated as the Japanese had learned how to fight the Mongols more effectively from their encounters in 1274. However, a storm hit, destroying one part of the fleet while scattering another part. Qubilai's efforts failed. Even without the *tsunami*, the Mongols would have found the conquest of Japan to be difficult.[52] This defeat marked the end of the Mongol Conquests, although Qubilai had other ideas. His advisors eventually persuaded him to abandon a third effort, due to the expense. While Qubilai's last foreign adventure in Java ended in military failure, it still yielded an immense amount of plunder. More importantly, his efforts in Southeast Asia opened commerce in the Indian Ocean. Before long, the primary trade and communications route between China and Persia was the sea route. Indeed, this is the route by which Marco Polo returned home rather than the land route.[53]

The Aftermath of Qubilai Khan

While Qubilai has been focused on foreign adventures, Qaidu had solidified his control in Central Asia and the Ilkhanids and Jochids continued their war. The Ilkhanids were never able to regain Syria permanently. Nor were the Mongols ever able to unite, although there was a brief period of *Pax Mongolica* when all of the Mongols recognized Temür Oljeitü (1295–1307) as the *khaghan*. This, however, only occurred after Qaidu had died in 1301. Even then unity proved fleeting. After Temur Oljeitü died divisions reoccurred and peace proved illusory.

The various Mongol states continued. Rather than a single hyper-power, four superpowers emerged. The Yuan Empire dominated East Asia until 1370, losing China to the nascent Ming dynasty in 1368. The Ilkhanate collapsed in 1335 due to a lack of male heirs. It splintered into a number of successor states, most led by Mongol military commanders. The Jochids finally conquered Azerbaijan in 1357, but then promptly lost it. It too gradually had split into a number of states by 1504. Lack of unity permitted the rise of Moscow which inexorably gobbled them up to create the Russian Empire. In Central Asia, the Ögödeid state was absorbed by the Chaghatayids. It remained a quasi-independent state after Qaidu's death for only a few years. The Chaghatayids also gradually fragmented. The rise of Tamerlane in Māwarānnahr ensured it would never be reunited.

Notes

[11] *The Secret History of the Mongols*, trans. and ed. Igor de Rachewiltz, 2 vols. (Leiden: Brill, 2004). Henceforth *SHM* and the citation number refers to passages, so that the reader may find the relevant passages in any translation.

[12] *SHM*, 62.

[13] *SHM*, 116–18; Paul Ratchnevsky, *Genghis Khan: His Life and Legacy* (Cambridge, MA: Blackwell, 1992), 34–47.

[14] *SHM*, 121.

[15] Ratchnevsky, 49–50; Zhao Gong, *Meng-Da Bei-Lu (Polnoe opisanie Mongolo-Tatar)*, trans. N. Ts. Munkuev (Moscow: Nauka, 1975), 49; Michal Biran, *Chinggis Khan* (London: OneWorld, 2007), 36.

[16] *SHM*, 129.

[17] *SHM*, 63–66, 73–75. Also see Isenbike Togan, *Flexibility & Limitation in Steppe Formations: The Kerait Khanate and Chinggis Khan* (Leiden: Brill, 1998), 80–92.

[18] *SHM*, 76–77.

[19] *SHM*, 84–86.

[20] *SHM*, 109–10; Togan, 107–8.

[21] *SHM*, 112–22.

[22] Anne Broadbridge, "Marriage, Family and Politics: The Ilkhanid-Oirat Connection," *Journal of the Royal Asiatic Society* 26, no. 2 (2016): 123n2.

[23] Michal Biran, *The Empire of the Qara Khitai in Eurasian History* (Cambridge: Cambridge University Press, 2005), 76.

[24] Muḥammad ibn Aḥmad al-Nasawī, *Sīrat al-Sulṭān Jalāl al-Dīn Mankubirtī* (Cairo: Dār al-Fikr al-'Arabī, 1953), 44–45.

[25] Rashīd al-Dīn indicates that Chinggis Khan did leave a small garrison. I suspect this to be a later event as no other sources support an occupation in 1210. See Rashiduddin Fazlullah, *Jami'u't-Tawarikh: Compendium of Chronicles*, trans. Wheeler M. Thackston (London: I. B. Tauris, 2012), 146; Rashīd al-Dīn, *Jāmi' al-tawārīkh*, ed. B. Karīmī (Tehran: Iqbal, 1983), 311.

[26] Paul Ratchnevsky, *Genghis Khan: His Life and Legacy* (Cambridge, MA: Blackwell, 1992), 108.

[27] "Shengwu Qin Zhenglu (Bogda Bagatur Bey-e-Ber Tayilagsan Temdeglel)," in *Bogda Bagatur Bey-e-Ber Tayilagsan Temdeglel*, ed. Asaraltu (Qayilar: Obor Monggol-un Soyul Keblel-un Qoriy-a, 1985), 46. Henceforth *SWQZL*.

[28] Ata-Malik Juvaini, *Genghis Khan: History of the World Conqueror*, trans. J. A. Boyle (Seattle: University of Washington Press, 1996), 65–66.

[29] *SWQZLU*, 51; Rashiduddin, trans. Thackston, 170–73.

[30] Juvaini, trans. Boyle, 105.

[31] Peter Jackson, *The Mongols and the Islamic World* (New Haven: Yale University Press, 2017), 155.

[32] Stephen Pow, "The Last Campaign and Death of Jebe Noyan," *Journal of the Royal Asiatic Society* 27, no. 1 (2017): 31–51.

[33] *SHM*, §268.

[34] *SHM*, §265.

[35] Juvaini, trans. Boyle, 452.

[36] Juvaini, trans. Boyle, 459; Bar Hebraeus, *The Chronography of Gregory Abu'l Faraj*, trans. Ernest A. Wallis Budge (Amsterdam: APA-Philo-Press, 1932), 396

[37] Sophia Menache, "Tartars, Jews, Saracens and the Jewish-Mongol 'Plot' of 1241," in *Travellers, Intellectuals, and the World Beyond Medieval Europe*, ed. James Muldoon (Malden: Ashgate, 2010), 260.

[38] John of Plano Carpini, "History of the Mongols," trans. a Nun of Stanbrook Abbey, in *The Mongol Mission*, ed. Christopher Dawson (Toronto: Toronto University Press, 1980), 65.

[39] Rashiduddin, trans. Thackston, 255; Rashīd al-Dīn, ed. Karīmī, 524.

[40] Hodong Kim, "A Reappraisal of Güyüg Khan," in *Mongols, Turks, and Others*, ed. Michal Biran and Reuven Amitai (Leiden: Brill), 317–19.

[41] Juvaini, trans. Boyle, 598–99.

[42] John Masson Smith, Jr. "Hülegü Moves West: High Living and Heartbreak on the Road to Baghdad," in *Beyond the Legacy of Genghis Khan*, ed. Linda Komaroff (Leiden: Brill, 2006), 111–134.

[43] Morris Rossabi, *Khubilai Khan: His Life and Times* (Berkeley: University of California Press, 2009), 45.

[44] Rashīd al-Dīn, ed. Karīmī, 617; Rashiduddin, trans. Thackston, 300; Rossabi, *Khubilai Khan*, 49.

[45] William of Rubruck in Dawson, *Mission*, 175; William of Rubruck, trans. Jackson, 209.

[46] Peter Jackson, "Dissolution of the Mongol Empire," *Central Asiatic Journal* (1978): 186–244, at 209.

[47] George Lane, *Early Mongol Rule in Thirteenth-Century Iran: A Persian Renaissance* (London: RoutledgeCurzon, 2003), 40.

[48] J. A. Boyle, "Dynastic and Political History of the Il-Khans," in *The Cambridge History of Iran*, ed. J. A. Boyle (Cambridge: Cambridge University Press, 1968), 353.

[49] Rashīd al-Dīn, ed. Karīmī, 678; Rashiduddin, trans. Thackston, 332.

[50] James P. Delgado, *Khubilai Khan's Lost Fleet* (Berkeley: University of California Press, 2008), 97; Randall J. Sasaki, *The Origins of the Lost Fleet of the Mongol Empire* (College Station: Texas A & M University Press, 2015), 34–41.

[51] Michael C. Brose, "Realism and Idealism in the '*yuanshi*': Chapters on Foreign Relations," *Asia Major*, 3rd ser., 19 (2006): 327–47.

[52] See Thomas D. Conlan, *In Little Need of Divine Intervention: Takezaki Suenaga's Scrolls of the Mongol Invasions of Japan*, Cornell East Asia Series (Ithaca: Cornell University East Asia Program, 2001).

[53] Polo, trans. Cliff, 12–14.

Chapter 2

The Mongol Military

The Venetian traveller Marco Polo wrote of the rise of the Mongols "[...] and when Chinggis Khan saw that he had so many people, he equipped them with bows and armor and went conquering through those other lands."[54] No one can discount the success of the Mongol military nor its importance in the creation of the Mongol Empire. It served not only as the instrument of conquest, but also the source of from which all other institutions originated. Yet, simply having a large number of men does not make a great army. Indeed, the term "horde" originates from the Mongolian word *ordo*. The latter refers to camp, but in English, it has become "horde", meaning a large group of people with a derogatory connotation, such as being unruly. It can also mean "an army or tribe of nomadic warriors."[55] Nonetheless, even in this example "horde" still has implications of being ill-disciplined and barbaric. Furthermore, it provides a completely inaccurate depiction of the Mongol military.

While it is sometimes thought that the Mongols conquered with overwhelming numbers, this is an inaccurate perception. At the time of the 1206 *quriltai,* the Mongol army probably numbered less than a hundred thousand men and the population of Mongolia may have numbered one million. Even today, with modern healthcare, the population of Mongolia is barely above three million.[56] Although Marco Polo unintentionally misleads us above, his next statement does bear some truth:

I tell you that they conquered a good 8 provinces but did them no harm, nor did he strip them of their things. But he took them with him to conquer other peoples. In this way, he conquered this great multitude of peoples, as you have heard.[57]

Marco Polo downplays the destructive nature of the Mongol armies (more on that later), and he is quite correct that the Mongols incorporated the defeated in to their armies. As mentioned previously, the defeated tribes of Mongolia were broken up and distributed into new regiments in order to form a single cohesive entity: the *Yeke Monggol Ulus.* Yet, not everyone became a Mongol. This privilege was restricted to the nomads. They received a unique haircut, reserved for Mongols, although there is some evidence that suggests that Chinggis Khan initially attempted to make everyone a Mongol.[58] The sedentary population, however, was ill-suited for transforming into nomadic horse archers. Instead, the Mongols allowed them to retain their own fighting methods and found ways of using them effectively in their military, whether as heavy cavalry or in siege warfare or in other novel techniques.

Training and Development
The Mongol military benefitted from a millennium's worth of steppe warfare and military practice. Since the time of the Scythians the combination of cavalry and composite bows have given the steppe nomads a considerable edge over other nomads. It provided them mobility that sedentary armies lacked as well as a considerable edge in weaponry. Other armies could assemble larger armies, but lacked the ability to compete with the nomads in terms of cavalry as they simply lacked the capability of producing a similar number of horses. Indeed, many states, including all of the dynasties of China imported horses from the steppes. In many respects, Chinggis Khan's greatest achievement was forging the disparate tribes of Mongolia into a single entity. In order to do this, however, he had to implement reforms that gave him an edge over the traditional forms of warfare commonly used in the

steppes, such as feigned retreats and double envelopment manoeuvres. The core of the Mongol military system developed during Chinggis Khan's rise to power.

Temüjin's time with Jamuqa served as an internship for military training. Normally, he would have learned this from his father, but Yesügei's murder robbed Temüjin of this experience. When he entered Toghril Ong-Khan's service as a *nökör*, Temüjin lacked crucial skills. After rescuing Börte he stayed with Jamuqa for an indeterminable amount of time. This was not simply a reunion with a childhood friend, but a mentoring program as Jamuqa not only served as Toghril's *nökör*, but also as a war leader.[59] In addition to the basics of warfare, Temüjin learned not only how to lead, but also how not to lead. This is evident from the number of people who left Jamuqa and entered Temüjin's service when he and Jamuqa parted ways. Although Jamuqa proved to be a fine military strategist, other facets of leadership eluded him. Temüjin's approach was different, particularly when dealing with the non-elites. Temüjin's own experience taught him that hardship happens and the quality of a person was of greater importance than their birthright. Thus, when it came to sharing the spoils of war, Temüjin tended to be more equitable than most.

Jamuqa's victory over Temüjin at the battle of Dalan Balzhut in 1187 demonstrated Temüjin still had much to learn in terms of military leadership. Yet, his absence from Mongolia after this defeat also demonstrates that he took that opportunity. While the *Mengda Beilu* hints he was in the Jin Empire in some capacity, it is possible, at some point during that ten-year absence, he received training of some form because he returned and became an excellent commander.[60] Furthermore, he also learned the value of loyalty and punishing those who were not. This became a hallmark of Mongol activity. Those who demonstrated loyalty were richly rewarded and those who were not faced severe consequences. This also applied to his enemies. On more than one occasion, Chinggis Khan executed those who took their leaders prisoner in order to curry favour.[61] His rationale was simple—if they did this once, how can I know they won't betray me? On the other hand, those who served their leader to the end of their capability garnered great respect for their loyalty. When those individuals entered his service, he ensured their position and also demonstrated his respect as in the case of Yelu Chucai who became one of the key members of the Mongol government.[62]

Chinggis Khan also emphasized talent over birthright. Many of these leading companions and generals came from the lower elements of society and indeed were crucial in developing a leadership cadre for the military. Two of the best-known examples were Sübedei and Jebe. Sübedei began his career as a household servant. He demonstrated his ability time and time again and eventually became the greatest general of the Mongol Empire, if not in world history. Jebe, another general, went from being an enemy warrior who almost killed Chinggis Khan to becoming a valued and talented commander for his ability as well as his bravado—Jebe demonstrated that he took responsibility for his actions and did not shirk the consequences.[63] Through his own experiences, Temüjin created a mentoring or intern system for his commanders. Just as he learned from Jamuqa and then perhaps while serving in the Jin Empire, he paired junior commanders with senior ones. Although Sübedei became a legend, he started with small units and gradually developed the ability to lead *minggans* or units of one thousand before leading a *tümen* or unit of ten thousand. Temüjin likewise paired his sons with commanders and sometimes with each other. For instance, Tolui received independent commands before his elder brothers Chaghadai and Ögödei as he demonstrated superior ability much earlier than either of them. Seniority was important, but not when lives were at stake.

Tactics and Strategies

Chinggis Khan adopted many traditional steppe forms of warfare. Besides tactics, he adopted the decimal system of organization, probably from the Kereit, which had been used since the time of the Xiongnu (200 BCE–91CE). Chinggis Khan refined traditional warfare by creating new formations and tactics that provided his armies distinct advantages over other nomads. The root of the system remained tied to traditional steppe warfare centred around horse archers, feigned retreats, arrow showers, and an emphasis on mobility and quick strikes. The new tactics and formations, however, relied on an increased discipline and training which also helped integrate the defeated nomads into the existing Mongol military units.[64] Of particular importance was an emphasis on transitioning from one formation to another, thus providing the Mongols the ability to adapt seamlessly to their opponent's formation.

Siege warfare developed slowly for the Mongols. Initially it consisted of blockades and simple attempts at storming cities through blunt force or deception. Gradually, however, the Mongols attracted individuals with expertise in siege warfare who not only taught them how to construct siege engines, such as trebuchets, but also how to use them effectively. Many of these individuals were deserters who joined the Mongols either because they had some grievance with their former employers or because they saw greater opportunities. Indeed, during the campaigns against the Jin Empire, a number of individuals joined the Mongols simply because the Mongols were winning.[65]

The Mongols also developed a strategy of conquest that permitted them to expand on multiple fronts without overextending themselves. I refer to this as the *tsunami* strategy as it resembles a tidal wave smashing the mainland, devastating a vast region, and then water recedes back into the ocean with only a portion remaining flooded.[66] In doing so, the Mongol armies destroyed all resistance in a region, particularly in terms of field armies. Should a few strongholds remain, these could then be isolated and reduced as needed. The Mongols did not attempt to directly control all of the areas they invaded. They occupied the strategic spaces—whether mountain passes, pastures, or trade routes. The devastated areas then served as buffers so that no one could attack the Mongols. Thus, the Mongols could station small armies, known as *tamma*, in the location and they served as highly mobile garrisons. These could respond to threats as needed, raid and intimate other areas, and perhaps even expand the area of Mongol control, but without requiring massive armies or infrastructure. Gradually, a civil administration filled in the conquered space, the occupational armies, the *tamma*, then moved to the new frontier or simply saw the territory under this military rule reduced.

Wrath of the Mongols

In addition to developing a well-organized and trained army, the Mongols enhanced their military's reputation through fear. Marco Polo is quite mistaken in claiming that Chinggis Khan's armies "did them no harm, nor did he strip them of their things."[67] Compare this with a statement by Chinggis Khan's contemporary, Ibn al-Athīr, who did not personally witness Chinggis Khan's invasion of Central Asia, but compiled his history based on reports from survivors:

> As for the Antichrist, he will spare those who follow him and destroy those who oppose him, but these did not spare anyone. On the contrary, they slew women, men and children. They split open the bellies of pregnant women and killed the foetuses. To God do we belong and to Him do we return. There is no power nor strength in God the High, the Mighty.
>
> This is the calamity whose sparks flew far and wide and whose damage was all-embracing. It spread through the lands like a cloud driven on by the wind, for a people emerged from the confines of China and made for the cities of Transoxiana, such as Samarqand, Bukhara and others. They took them and treated their inhabitants as we shall recount. A group of them then crossed into Khurasan and thoroughly dealt with it, conquering, destroying, slaughtering and plundering. Then they passed on to Rayy and Hamadhan, the Uplands and cities up to the boundary of Iraq. Subsequently they attacked Azerbayjan and Arran, which they ruined and most of whose people they killed.

Only the rare fugitive survived. [All this was] in less than a year. Nothing like this had ever been heard of.[68]

Ibn al-Athīr is but one individual who reported the Mongol onslaught in apocalyptic terms. As Peter Jackson has conclusively demonstrated, destruction caused by the Mongol invasions under Chinggis Khan was immense in terms of not only lives, but also property; the sources, however, cannot be taken literally.[69] Although the Mongols may not have killed two million people at Herat (it is doubtful that the Herat and the surrounding region supported that many people in the thirteenth century), we can, however believe that the destruction caused by the Mongols as well as the fury with which they attacked was unlike anything that the region had ever experienced.

The Middle East had long experienced the entrance of nomads from the steppes, but the violence unleashed by the Mongols was new and at unprecedented levels, causing the chroniclers to view them less as human and more as a force of nature or even the judgement of god. Only through death could one escape their wrath. The Persian chronicler Jūzjānī fled from the Mongols to the safety of Delhi in India and recorded an incident that a caravan from the Khwārazmian Empire witnessed in the Jin Empire when they came to Zhongdu to conduct business:

> On reaching the gate of the city of [Zhongdu], we perceived, in a place under a bastion of the citadel, an immense quantity of bones collected. Inquiry was made and people replied, that, on the day the city was captured, 60,000 young girls, virgins, threw themselves from this bastion of the fortress and destroyed themselves, in order that they might not fall captives into the hands of the [Mongol] forces, and that all these were their bones.[70]

If true, these women had good reason for their mass suicide. In addition to the sheer destruction and slaughter, the Mongols also removed people from localities. Women could expect to be raped and many were carried off to become slaves. Townspeople of all types were forced to fight alongside, or rather in front of, the Mongols. These "lucky" members of the arrow fodder brigade carried debris to be thrown into moats and trenches at the next location that the Mongols attacked. They also served as human shields as their presence and function meant that the Mongols did not have to venture too close to the walls until a breach occurred. Failure by the arrow fodder brigade to fulfil their duties meant death. At the same time, the defenders on the walls undoubtedly shot people they knew as neighbours, which must have been detrimental to morale.

Those not serving in this capacity were sorted into categories. Those with useful skills, such as artisans, found themselves removed to Mongolia or the camp of a Mongol prince. There they made goods for the Mongols, including weaponry, armour, and siege engines such as the Chinese and Central Asians captured during the conquests of Chinggis Khan. The Mongols sent them to central Mongolia where they became the population of Chinqai Balasaghun, or Chinqai City. Chinqai, an official in the Mongol Empire, developed this settlement to serve as an industrial centre. A silversmith from Paris who was captured in Hungary found himself in Qaraqorum, the Mongol capital, where he created an ingenious drinking fountain that served *kara kumiss* (distilled fermented mare's milk), wine, mead, and rice wine.[71] German miners captured in Poland worked mines in the Tien Shan Mountains in modern Kyrgyzstan.[72] While not pleasant, having useful skills increased one's chance at surviving.

Thus, while Marco Polo is a valuable source, one must always question his veracity. Indeed, much of Qubilai Khan's fame in the west came directly from Marco Polo who only had positive things to say, which contrasts greatly with Jūzjānī who never had a kind word for the Mongols. Indeed, Jūzjānī refers to Chinggis Khan as "The Accursed." Yet, all sources must be read with a critical eye. The story about the virgins leaping to their death probably did not happen. Although Jūzjānī learned of it from another Khwārazmian refugee who had served in the court, there is evidence that the mentioned caravaneer was in the employ of Chinggis Khan.[73] The Mongols used many merchants in espionage, not only to gather information but also to sow disinformation. Furthermore, the story gained credence because people could and wanted to believe terrible things associated with the Mongols. The Mongols had no compunction about discouraging this idea; fear was their ally.

The Mongols' initial diplomacy was simple: submit or die. Those that submitted without resistance were treated well. Those that resisted faced a merciless foe. When news of this spread, and reinforced by stories of Mongol atrocities, many towns submitted quickly. From these the Mongols expected tribute, supplies, and troops when requested. Some of those that submitted later rebelled. Rebels faced total destruction.

Ideology

The Mongols' Manichean approach was based on the final element of their military success: ideology. The Mongols did not just wantonly strike out across Eurasia in lust of rape, pillage, and plunder. Chinggis Khan's early motivations were to secure his nascent *Yeke Monggol Ulus* by eliminating threats from nomadic rivals and then by avenging past wrongs against the Jin Empire, who also had a habit of meddling in steppe affairs (to ensure no one could threaten North China). The Mongols entered Central Asia not for conquest but because of a trade dispute. Yet, their success and the brilliance of Chinggis Khan's reign demonstrated to them that Köke Möngke Tengri, the Blue Eternal Sky or Heaven favoured them. By the reign of Ögödei, it was clear that Heaven had decreed that Chinggis Khan and his heirs should rule the world. Those who did not submit violated the will of Heaven. Thus, any ruler or city that resisted the Mongols was a rebel, not only against the Mongols, but against the will of Heaven. The only recourse was destruction. Their conquests were not only ones of world domination, but were ones of a holy war. The only tenet was to accept Mongol rule.

Notes

54 Marco Polo, *The Description of the World* (Indianapolis: Hackett, 2016), 52.

55 "Horde," https://en.oxforddictionaries.com/definition/horde. Accessed June 1, 2018.

56 "Mongolia," *The World Factbook* https://www.cia.gov/library/publications/the-world-factbook/geos/mg.html. Accessed June 1, 2018.

57 Polo, trans. Cliff, 52.

58 John of Plano Carpini in Dawson, *Mission*, 32–33; William of Rubruck in Dawson, *Mission*, 101–2; William of Rubruck, trans. Jackson, 88.

59 See Timothy May, "Jamuqa and the Education of Chinggis Khan," *Acta Mongolica* 6 (2006): 273–86.

60 Zhao Gong, *Meng-Da Bei-Lu*, 39.

61 Rachewiltz, *Secret History*, 129.

62 Igor de Rachewiltz, "Yeh-Lü Ch'u-Ts'ai (1189–1243), Yeh-Lü Chu (1221–1285)," in *In the Service of the Khan,* ed. Igor de Rachewilz, Hok-lam Chan, Hsiao Ch'i-ch'ing, and Peter Geier (Wiesbaden: Harrassowitz, 1993), 140.

63 Rachewiltz, *Secret History*, 68–69.

64 For more on formations and training see May, *The Mongol Art of War*.

65 Thomas Allsen, "The Rise of the Mongolian Empire and Mongolian Rule in North China," in *The Cambridge History of China*, vol. 6, *Alien Regimes and Border States, 907–1368*, ed. Herbert Franke and Denis Twitchett (Cambridge: Cambridge University Press, 1994), 358.

66 See Timothy May, "Mongol Conquest Strategy in the Middle East," in *Mongols' Middle East: Continuity and Transformation in Ilkhanid Iran*, ed. Bruno De Nicola and Charles Melville (Leiden: Brill, 2016), 11–37; May, "The Mongol Art of War and the Tsunami Strategy [Монгольское искусство войны и стратегия цунами]," Золотоордынская цивилизация. Научный ежегодник [Golden Horde Civilization. Research Annual], Выпуск 8, Казань: Институт истории им. Ш.Марджани АН РТ, 8 (2015): 31–37; May, "Grand Strategy in the Mongol Empire," *Acta Historica Mongolici* 16 (2017): 78–105.

67 Polo, trans. Cliff, 52.

68 Ibn Al-Athir, *The Chronicle of Ibn al-Athīr for the Crusading Period from al-Kāmil fī'l-ta'rīkh. Part 3: The Years 589–629/1193–1231: The Ayyubids after Saladin and the Mongol Menace*, trans. D. S. Richards (Burlington: Ashgate, 2008).

[69] Peter Jackson, *The Mongols and the Islamic World* (New Haven: Yale University Press, 2017), 153–81.

[70] Minhāj al-Dīn Jūzjānī, *Ṭabakāt-i-Nāṣirī* (Kolkata: Asiatic Society, 2010), 965.

[71] William of Rubruck in Dawson, *Mission*, 157, 176; William of Rubruck, trans. Jackson, 183, 209.

[72] William of Rubruck in Dawson, *Mission*, 135–36; William of Rubruck, trans. Jackson, 146–47.

[73] Jūzjānī, 102.

Chapter 3

The Mongol Government

While the Mongol military's role in their success is undeniable, both in terms of conquest and then retaining control, it was but one facet of the Mongol government, albeit the core to that institution. The Mongol civil administration also proved to be effective and innovative. This chapter will not be a detailed study of institutions and governmental structures—there are plenty of discussions to be found in the Further Reading section. Rather, we will discuss the philosophical underpinnings of Mongol rule and the implementation of those ideas. This philosophy and conception of rule was fundamental to Mongol success, at least in the short term.

The *Altan Urugh* (the Family of Chinggis Khan) at the Top of the Hierarchy

The government existed of several often-overlapping layers, each tied to the overriding conception of Mongol authority. The overlapping layers of authority both served to extend Mongol rule, while also placing limitations on individual power. The *khaghan* reigned at the top, but no matter who sat on the throne, the *khaghan* was never autocratic. The Mongol ruler had to weigh the interests of several factions. As Chinggis Khan had eliminated or diminished competing aristocracies, the *altan urugh* (Golden Kin) or the family of Chinggis Khan resided at the top of the hierarchy. As indicated in the previous chapter, the Mongols came to believe that the *Möngke*

Köke Tengri had bequeathed the world to Chinggis Khan and his descendants. As such, it is not surprising that the *altan urugh* viewed the Mongol Empire as a sort of family business and they were the shareholders. While the idea of the Will of Heaven surely reinforced this view, it is clear that the preeminence of the *altan urugh* originated during Chinggis Khan's lifetime. He intended that his family (his descendants and those of his brothers) would be the aristocracy, replacing other lineages that existed in the steppes previously, as is shown when he assigned territories and people to his family.[74]

Although it is not clear how large Chinggis Khan originally intended the appanages to be, after his death these patrimonies became better defined with most of the empire apportioned among the *altan urugh.* Not only did this provide territory and pastures for the flocks and herds of the *altan urugh*, but it also spread the relatives of Chinggis Khan across the empire so that the majority of the empire had members of the *altan urugh* in the vicinity. The system of allotting the *altan urugh* patrimonies was not perfect. Spreading the royal family throughout the empire, however, also carried risk as the distance could potentially make them territorial and focused on their own local interests rather than the empire as a whole.

To mitigate the possibility of the empire fracturing along territorial interests, members also received *qubi*, or shared revenue. Thus, a grandson of Jochi living along the Dnieper River could still receive revenue from the workshops of a city in China. Conversely, the sons of Chinggis Khan's brothers in Manchuria might receive income from the markets in Iran. A network of distribution ensured that members of the *altan urugh* received their shares and kept them informed of events. Not everything was shared equally as the system was based on the importance of individuals, but it did help maintain a sense of shared interest and furthering the view that the empire itself was truly a family business. The *altan urugh* also took precautions to safeguard their interests and prevent others from usurping their prerogatives. The best example of this came from Chinggis Khan's lifetime.

Chinggis Khan came to appreciate that as long as there were competing aristocracies, stability was impossible in the steppes. Thus, as he defeated his enemies, he eliminated the aristocracy—killing off the males and distributing the elite women among his sons and followers. Thus, in the new aristocracy, one's connection to Chinggis Khan determined one's status. This included not only his sons, but also his brothers. He also prioritized his sons by their mother, thus those born from Börte, his first and primary wife, had higher standing than those from other wives.

Although appreciative of meritocracy, Chinggis Khan came to realize that some ranking was necessary as he learned from his experience with his stepbrother, Kököchü, also known as the shaman Teb Tengri. Mönglik, Teb Tengri's father, and a former *nökör* of Yesügei married Hö'elün, thus making his sons (from a previous wife) Chinggis Khan's step-brothers. Although Temüjin distributed troops and people to Mönglik and his sons, Teb Tengri yearned for more power and insinuated that Jochi Qasar, Chinggis Khan's brother, would eventually seize power. While Hö'elün prevented Chinggis Khan from executing his brother, he still stripped him of followers.[75] When Teb Tengri and his brothers began to impose on Chinggis Khan's youngest brother, Temüge, Börte became involved and said:

> They recently ganged up and beat Qasar. And now, why do they make this Otčigin kneel down behind them? What kind of behavior is this?[...] How will people covertly injuring in this fashion your younger brothers, *who are* like cypresses and pines, *ever* allow my three or four little "naughty ones" to govern while they are *still* growing up? What are those Qongqotan doing? *Now* that you have let them *ill*-treat your younger brothers in such a way, how do you view *all this*?[76]

Börte's admonishment awakened Chinggis Khan to the threat to his power. Chinggis Khan did not want his brothers' status to be solely based on kinship, but also through their own merit. Mönglik's marriage to mother Hö'elün, however, now connected the Qongqotan clan to him and unintentionally introduced a new element that served as an avenue to power not only by becoming step-brothers, but also by Chinggis Khan's sometimes tenuous relationship with his brothers. Teb Tengri was executed as a dire warning to Mönglik's remaining sons and put them in their place. Thereafter, only those directly related to Chinggis Khan had power as the *altan urugh*.

The sons and brothers of Chinggis Khan were not the only members of the *altan urugh*. Chinggis Khan also had several daughters who played important parts in the establishment of the Mongol Empire. Indeed, the Mongol queens and princesses were instrumental throughout the history of the empire.[77] Although the patrimonies were the domains of the male members of the *altan urugh*, females accessed territory and power through other means.

Chinggis Khan's daughters married into the families of rulers who submitted to Chinggis Khan, a practice that continued after his death. These marriage alliances (*quda*) also made the daughter or sister the Khan's representative at that court. In many instances, the female Chinggisid served as a viceroy, officially or unofficially. They also returned to the Mongol court from time to time in order to renew their ties to the Mongol Empire. In some situations, it helped cement ties between nomadic tribes so that certain groups became regular sources of brides for the Chinggisid princes, such as the Oirat and the Onggirad. In other situations, the marriage of the non-nomadic ruler to a Chinggisid bride raised their status as the husband became *güregen* or a son-in-law of the *khaghan*. This elevated the husband into an elite circle just below the *altan urugh*, yet the connection remained through their wives.

The *Noyad*, the Major Military Commanders, and the *Keshig* Bodyguard

Chinggis Khan designed his empire, nonetheless, with a clear demonstration that he did not fully trust his relatives (brothers or sons). He assigned individuals to advise and watch them. In part, this served as a mentoring system and perhaps a Mongol derivative from the Turkic *atabeg* practice, in which the sons were trained by a non-relative on how to rule in a distant province. His major military commanders or *noyad* (sing. *noyan*) were all non-relatives and in many cases received commands that exceeded the allotment of people given to his family.[78] Indeed, while Mongol princes could command armies, the *khaghan* assigned generals, thus ensuring that the military remained in the hands of the ruler. As the empire grew, the major princes, particularly the senior member of the four princely households (Jochids, Chaghatayids, Ögödeids, and Toluids) developed their own armies, but the imperial household possessed not only the largest *keshig*, but also access to the leading generals. These commanders tended to be vested in the success of the empire rather than a particular khan. Furthermore, their success gave them access to the *khaghan* to an extent that paralleled that of the *altan urugh*.

These *noyad* achieved their positions based on loyalty and merit. Chinggis Khan possessed a keen eye for talent and promoted individuals regardless of their previous positions. Thus former slaves and commoners were elevated to lead units and were gradually promoted to command larger units as they demonstrated their competency. The *noyad* commanders were among Chinggis Khan's most trusted assistants, even more so than family members. Bound by the common experience of travails during Temüjin's rise to power, they became the foundation that supported the throne of Chinggis Khan. His appreciation of their loyalty and service also made them richly rewarded, sometimes given tax immunities or even immunity from punishment. So grateful was he that Chinggis Khan sometime extended these benefits to their offspring.[79] Their sons were also enrolled into the *keshig*.

The *keshig* served not only as a bodyguard, but also was the basis of the early Mongol administration. Chinggis Khan's sons would also form their own smaller version of the *keshig*, which then formed the basis of their rule in their own territories. It was through their service to the *khaghan* that individuals were selected, appointed on merit to serve as *tammachin*, *jarquchin* (judges), and *daruqachin* (governors).

While members might leave the *keshig*, it was a temporary assignment and they never lost their membership. This created a dual-government in which the military administration overlapped with the civil administration. Yet not all of the officials came from the *keshig*. Most of the bureaucracy came from without.

The Civil Government and Fiscal Districts

The Mongol civil government gradually governed pacified regions. In the past, scholars believed the Mongols took a half-hearted interest in actually ruling the sedentary regions and relied heavily on sedentary officials (Chinese, Persians, Uyghurs, and others). While they did rely heavily on non-nomadic personnel, the Mongols did in fact take a great interest in ruling their empire. Sedentary personnel were necessary not only for their expertise but also for their numbers as the empire was too vast to be governed solely by Mongols. If local rulers submitted properly they retained their positions, although with a *daruqachi* or Mongol governor or agent present. Where the *daruqachi* did not directly rule, he acted as liaison between the locality and the imperial government. In many cases, the Mongol *daruqachi* was not an actual Mongol or even a member of the *keshig*, but a local who entered Mongol service. Local rulers who resisted were replaced by compliant relatives or eradicated, as in the case of the Tangut royalty who initially submitted and then rebelled. While Mongol princes expressed their wishes within their patrimonies, their authority often vied with that of imperial officials such as a *jarquchi* or judge and high governor who served as the emperor's direct representative.

In addition to the central administration, the Mongols also created fiscal districts, which often overlapped the appanages of the *altan urugh*. These fiscal districts, first created by Ögödei, primarily comprised sedentary regions: North China, Turkestan, and Khurāsān.[80] During Möngke's reign, the Rus' territories were added. By having the fiscal districts overlap the *altan urugh*'s appanages, the central government

inserted another layer of control over them by having imperial officials present. The fiscal aspect also ensured that taxes
were sent to the capital, Qaraqorum, thus preventing any individual member of the *altan urugh* from becoming wealthier
than the central government and suborned the resources of
the empire to the central government. While the *altan urugh*
were the elite of the empire, the multiple layers of authority
diluted their power as well as that of the *noyad* to prevent
any individual from attempting to secede from the empire.
At the same time, it also gave the princes enough autonomy
to have some independence of action, but at a level that was
acceptable to the central government.

The attempt to centralize authority was a slow process.
The root of central authority in the Mongol empire can be
traced to Chinggis Khan's goal to create a single identity—a
bit of a novel concept in an era where nationalism did not
exist. Steppe confederations and tribes in general were
known by their dominant element. While it was impossible
to completely eradicate other tribal identities, Chinggis Khan
made a good effort by using decimal organization. The decimal system was not new to the steppes and had been used
by the Xiongnu and numerous polities afterwards. Yet, unlike
the other groups, Chinggis Khan used it not only for military
formations but also as a principle of organization. For military
units, defeated tribes were then dispersed into the military
units without the option of ever transferring. Chinggis Khan
intended to prevent them from ever assembling again in a
coherent group. Those who were loyal to Chinggis Khan kept
their people intact. When the Kereit were defeated, they were
one of the few groups who maintained a coherent identity,
but that was largely because Temüjin had prior history with
them and their war was not due to an existing feud, but rather
animosity and jealousy that arose in the leadership of the
Kereit. Chinggis Khan did not eliminate all of the Kereit leadership either, only those that had been the cause of the conflict. He then also married the Kereit daughters into his family
to bind the Kereit closer to them. Although the process was
not perfect and many tribal names still appear today in the

regions of the former Mongol Empire, Chinggis Khan did truly forge a new Mongol identity during the wars of unification.

Successive *khaghans* gradually implemented policies that centralized authority while attempting to balance the various layers of power throughout the empire. Möngke's reign was the pinnacle of centralized authority, aided by a purge of the *altan urugh* and the *noyad* affiliated with the Ögödeid and Chaghatayid families. The establishment of strong institutions and the overlapping of institutions allowed the Mongol Empire to survive during periods of turmoil. The institutions of central authority, however, never had solid enough foundations to survive all threats to unity. Still, they laid a basis that permitted the Mongol Empire to expand and implement policies that fuelled their success.

Notes

74 Rachewiltz, *Secret History*, 166–67.

75 Rachewiltz, *Secret History*, 170–71.

76 Rachewiltz, *Secret History*, 171–72.

77 See Anne Broadbridge, *Women and the Making of the Mongol Empire* (Cambridge: Cambridge University Press, 2018).

78 Rachewiltz, *Secret History*, 166–68.

79 Rachewiltz, *Secret History*, 142–52.

80 Thomas T. Allsen, *Mongol Imperialism: The Policies of the Grand Qan Möngke in China, Russia, and the Islamic Lands, 1251–1259* (Berkeley: University of California Press, 1987), 101.

Chapter 4

Policies

The policies of the Mongols were as important as the actual institutions of their government as they dictated not only the Mongols' actions and their view of the world, but also how others interacted with them as neighbours or subjects. What follows discusses the general policies of the Mongols. Exceptions can always be found but the following suffices to give a sense of how the Mongols operated.

The Will of Heaven

Militarily and diplomatically, the Mongols had a very narrow sense of the world. As they believed that *Köke Möngke Tengri* or the Blue Eternal Heaven had bequeathed the world to Chinggis Khan and his successors for them to rule it, therefore all peoples should submit before the Mongols. Failure to do so meant that they were in violation with the will of Heaven and thus a rebel. On this matter, there was no discussion. Various khans provided evidence to why this point was non-negotiable, such as the size of their empire and whom they defeated—if not for the will of Heaven, then how could this have been achieved?[81] Thus while some observers found them arrogant, the Mongols also possessed a sense of awe for their accomplishments and expected others to accept what they viewed as self-evident truths. As a result, before the Mongols invaded a kingdom, they sent envoys who gave the ruler very simple terms which equated to "submit or die."

There was no third course of action. Attempts to negotiate terms did not go over well and may have been viewed as an effort to stall or as a passive form of resistance. Indeed, those who did resist would be destroyed, and usually the more determined the resistance, the greater the level of destruction by the Mongols. Those who harmed the Mongols' envoys could expect no mercy.

These policies contributed to the Mongols' success in a number of ways. First, the ideology of Heaven's Decree assisted in providing legitimacy to Chinggisid rule and a counter to the claims of other authorities, such as China's own Heaven's Mandate, the authority of the Abbasid Caliph, and that of the Pope. The Mongols did not appeal to a higher power—that power had chosen them. It is doubtful if this idea manifested during Chinggis Khan's reign as he did seek to conquer the world. It did, however, assist Ögödei and fuel the continued momentum of the Mongols. For the nomads they conquered, it was part of the continued policy of transforming them into Mongols—those that did not accept the Mongol world view were seen as slaves who needed to be brought to heel. Secondly, and perhaps an unintended effect, in a world in which apocalyptic prophecies were common, this idea not only assisted the Mongols in rationalizing their success, but the conquered were able to justify the conquests as well. It also helped fuel an almost holy war approach to the Mongols conquest.

Diplomatically it provided a clear Mongol ideology on how to view the world. This simple view of "surrender or die," however, belied a more nuanced approach. While the Mongols did adhere to the idea of the Will of Heaven, their diplomacy produced results. Those who chose to surrender allowed the Mongols to add to the empire quite effectively and without violence. Those who resisted allowed the Mongols to prioritize and focus their forces. But what about those who were non-committal? It allowed the Mongols to prevaricate. If the noncommittal ruler sent presents to the Mongol ruler or envoys, the Mongols could use the fiction that they submitted and delay dealing with them until more suitable opportunities arose. If a potentate did none of these actions, the Mongols had *casus belli*—not only to justify the war to themselves, but in conversations with other rulers. These situations then became examples for other rulers as demonstrated when Hülegü wrote to King Louis IX of France in 1262:

> A few years later, by virtue of the living God we sent our proposal first to the Sultan Hassan of the Assassins, that is the knife-murderers, to signify that in view of the considerations touched upon he should be prompt to accept our rule. However he was confident in his strongholds that were sited on the tops of mountains and he believed his army to be sufficiently large, so he dared to join battle with us, but we wiped him and his tribe from the face of the earth and razed to the foundations his strongest castles, Baymundeu and Alamut as well as about 50 others. When this had been completed, we sent the above-mentioned order to the fourteen kings and princes of the knife-murderers who also disobeyed our commands, with the result that they too were slaughtered with all their troops in the same manner. A short while after we had accomplished this we decided the original order we had sent to the above-mentioned should be sent to the caliph of Baldach. He ridiculously boasted that as a descendant of Mahomet, the unspeakable pseudo-prophet of the Saracens, he was the pope and head of the world, and he did not hesitate to insist that the Almighty Creator had created the heavens, the earth and everything in it for the said Mahomet and his people only. Trusting hugely in his own high magnificence, his countless wealth, castles and troops he chose to join battle with us rather than meekly obey our orders. We defeated him just like all the others in open combat, killing two thousand thousand of his men and a host of others too many to count.[82]

For subjects, the Mongol policy was quite clear: if you submitted, you were expected to send tribute, should formally submit to the ruler, and provide troops and supplies (food, horses, etc.) when requested. The Mongols viewed failure in fulfilling these obligations as an act of rebellion. Those that submitted willingly often found their lands increased and presented with honours. Those that rebelled experienced punishment of varying levels. Some regions that rebelled frequently experienced direct Mongol rule or a change in dynasty. The Mongols often kept hostages, not so much to ensure good behaviour, but rather as an opportunity to groom and observe potential replacements. Loyal rulers sometimes were even rewarded with a Chinggisid princess. While it marked the *khaghan*'s esteem, such a marriage alliance also placed a Mongol princess in a position to help guide the ruler and ensure their loyalty to the Mongols. Any harm to the princess risked severe retaliation.

Religious Policies

The Mongols also took a very practical stance on religion during the period of the *Yeke Monggol Ulus* (1206–1260)—practise your religion, do not impose it on others. As long as you did not cause trouble, such as starting religious feuds, or similar, the Mongols simply did not care about your personal faith. This was not a new innovation by the Mongols and appears to have been an Inner Asian trait.[83] One should not mistake this for a modern or perhaps a twentieth-century sense of toleration (I'm not willing to give the twenty-first century the benefit of the doubt yet). Clergy also received immunity from taxation, although not all were included. The Mongols favoured clergy out of respect for their profession and expected the clergy to offer prayers to their respective divine beings on behalf of the *khaghan*. While the Mongols may not have subscribed to a particular religion, they saw no need to offend gods either. At the same time, not all religions were treated equally.

Jews, Zoroastrians, and Manicheans did not experience the same level of privilege as Buddhists, Daoists, Muslims, and Christians. Whereas the clergy of the latter four experienced immunity from taxation, the former three did not. Part of this appears to be that they lacked any rulers or large populations. Another factor may be that they had no representatives among the Mongols to press for these advantages.[84] Daoists earned early favour through Changzi, who impressed Chinggis Khan, and Buddhists also found highly placed individuals such as Yelu Chucai to advocate for them. Despite his destruction of the Khwārazmian state, Chinggis Khan did not have any overt bias against Muslims. Indeed, he had trusted companions who were Muslims and promoted many others to high positions within the administration. Christians also found favour particularly through the Nestorian Christians among the Mongol elite, such as among the Kereit, Naiman, and Önggüd. Unfortunately, Jews, Zoroastrians, and Manicheans never found such support, thus the Mongols lacked any incentive to curry their favour. Had they have constituted more of a political force (within or without the Mongol government), it is likely that the Mongols would have extended them privileges similar to those other groups. This is what happened with Confucianism. Originally, Confucianism was in this category, but after Chinggis Khan's death, it gradually gained the same privileges as the "Big Four."

The Mongol policies regarding religion benefitted their empire in numerous ways. The first is that it prevented religious strife and thus persecution. This is not to say the Mongol system was perfect, as persecution did occur, although it is not always clear whether it was state instigated or simply coincidental.[85] Additionally, it permitted the Mongols to show favour to all religions. Thus, rulers could take part or witness rituals by all of the religions within their empire. Certain rulers might favour one religion, but even this is somewhat difficult to determine as observers often judged favouritism not so much as what they did for one religion as what they didn't do. An example would be if Muslims viewed the Mongols as favouring Christians if they abolished the *jizya* or poll tax or Christians might view the Mongols as favouring Muslims or Buddhists if they did not convert to Christianity. Equally interesting is that virtually all of the missionaries who flocked to Qaraqorum hoping to convert the khan came away with a sense that the khan would convert to their respective religion very soon. In short, the missionaries always found what they were looking for, both positive and negative. In many ways, the Mongols were religious chameleons, flexible in their approach and neutral to keep most religious devotees interested in them. Most viewed the Mongols as infidels, but then found ways to accommodate living under infidel rule. The other factor is that because of their religious neutrality, it permitted them to better use the resources for their armies. They did not exclude groups based on religious identity as occurred in the Muslim and Christian worlds. The Mongols focused on ability and became adept at playing groups off each other so that no single group dominated the empire, other than the Mongols. Their neutrality in religion also allowed the Mongol identity to remain the key component of empire rather than any particular religion or other belief system.

Commercial Policies

The Mongols achieved success in their commercial policies, which enhanced and funded the expansion of the Mongol Empire. From the beginning, the Mongols were interested in trade. While their wars with Xi Xia and the Jin Empire were not directly related to trade concerns, the Mongols did promote treaties that provided tribute and thus income to the empire. The Khwārazmian War, however, began precisely due to a trade dispute. Before long, the Mongols dominated much of the network of trade routes known as the Silk Road. While these routes facilitated trade, they were also the main lines of communication and easiest routes for armies as well. The conquests benefitted from controlling trade routes, but there is little evidence that this was a primary goal of Mongol expansion. Indeed, the fact that they never attempted to conquer Constantinople demonstrates that controlling trade routes were never a critical part of Mongol policy.

The policies that did promote commercial activity came from many areas and all of these reduced the cost of trade. The first is that the Mongols ensured security along the trade routes. Bandits were eliminated when possible and the Mongol troops patrolled the routes. It was said that a virgin with a pot filled with treasure could walk from one end of the empire to the other.[86] While this example is hyperbole, nonetheless it conveys the idea that safety along the trade routes had greatly improved under the Mongols. Furthermore, the Mongols reduced the tariffs and taxes that merchants paid, not only through policy, but through conquest. Their policy was to introduce the *tamgha*, which became a sort of Value-Added Tax or tariff that merchants paid. They received documentation with a stamp indicating that the *tamgha* had been paid and did not pay it again while in the empire. At a modest five percent it remained quite reasonable. In addition, Mongol security cut the costs of security. Guards were still necessary, but one did not need as many. Furthermore, the Mongol conquests eliminated many tariffs as the Mongols eradicated independent kingdoms that collected them. Previously, merchants often had to pay tariffs almost every time they crossed a border. This obstacle was removed once the borders disappeared. To be sure, the system was not perfect as no society or state has ever eliminated graft. Still, the Mongols set the conditions for commercial success.

Additional commercial success came through the actions of Ögödei. While the Mongol khans remained nomadic in the Orkhon Valley and did not actually reside in a capital city, they still built one. Qaraqorum, however, was largely a place for the Mongols to keep their stuff. With an empire the size of the Mongol Empire, a capital was necessary even though it went contrary to the policies of traditional nomadic empires that eschewed cities as it made them vulnerable by being stationary. Diplomats, envoys, and others, however, needed a destination where they could execute their duties and the Mongol bureaucracy needed a location to their jobs. While high-ranking ministers might travel with the court, low-ranking functionaries still had to carry out the ubiquitous tasks of running the state. Thus, a city was built. Merchants supplied the city and conducted business—with individuals coming from across the empire, commerce flourished.

Qaraqorum, however, was not exactly on one of the main trade routes. Ögödei, however, found a way to change this. Much to the chagrin of his treasury officials and ministers of finance, Ögödei often paid double for merchandise, no matter the quality. While the sources portray him as profligate and perhaps a bit nutty in his spending, Ögödei's purpose was to attract merchants—like flies to honey:

> When he seated himself upon the throne of kingship and the fame of his kindness and generosity was spread throughout the world, merchants began to come to his Court from every side, and whatever goods they had brought, whether good or bad, he would command them to be brought at the full price. And it usually happened that without casting a glance at their wares or inquiring the price he would give them all away.[87]

Success was immediate. Soon merchants from across Eurasia ventured to Qaraqorum. Other cities also arose. In the west, Batu built Sarai for the same purpose, although it was more accessible from the main trade routes. Nonetheless, his effort to promote commerce succeeded. Güyük continued his father's policies. Merchants also found benefits from the *altan urugh* by forming *ortoq* relationships in which the *altan urugh* invested capital in caravans or loaned money to merchants at a low interest rate. With the additional capital as well as the important ties, these merchants experienced tremendous success and the economy of the empire flourished.

While Ögödei's policies caused anxiety among his ministers, they also ensured that commerce thrived and that wealth circulated throughout the empire rather than remaining locked in the Khan's coffers. Undoubtedly, not everyone saw the fruit of such policies. Nonetheless, long-distant merchants needed food, lodging, and beasts of burden for the trek to Mongolia. Luxury goods such as silk, furs, and spices gained wider circulation and found new markets, as did everyday items such as chickpeas, wool, and feathers for arrow fletching.

Mongol success cannot be simply explained through military superiority. As stated early, it is one thing to conquer an empire, it is another to rule it. The fact that the empire survived the death of Chinggis Khan and then continued to expand is a testament not only to the Mongol military, but also to the Mongol administration. While rebellions did occur, the fact that they were not widespread demonstrates that the Mongols found other means of mitigating rebellion besides brute force. Rebellions were localized and rarely gained traction. While the Mongols will never be accused of pandering to their subjects, they did take steps to ensure the peace such as taking a largely neutral stance in terms of religion and focusing on ability rather than religious or ethnic abilities. Finally, their commercial policies permitted trade to grow which also facilitated the recovery of many areas that had once been devastated by the Mongols.

Notes

[81] Rachewiltz, *Secret History*, 168, 176; also see Shagdaryn Bira, "Mongolian Tenggerism and Modern Globalism: A Retrospective Outlook on Globalization," *Journal of the Royal Asiatic Society*, 3rd ser., 14 (2004): 3–12; Herbert Franke, "From Tribal Chieftain to Universal Emperor and God: The Legitimation of the Yüan Dyansty," in *China Under Mongol Rule* (Burlington: Ashgate, 1994), 3–85; Reuven Amitai, *Holy War and Rapprochement* (Turnhout: Brepols, 2013). These are but a sampling of scholarly works examining this issue.

[82] Hülegü, "Hulegu, Mongol Il-Khan of Persia, to Louis IX, King of France (1262). Maragha," 156–160, in *Letters from the East: Crusaders, Pilgrims and Settlers in the 12th–13th Centuries*, trans. Malcolm Barber and Keith Bate (Burlington: Ashgate, 2010), 157–58.

[83] Michal Biran, *The Empire of the Qara Khitai in Eurasian History* (Cambridge: Cambridge University Press, 2005), 180–191.

[84] Christopher P. Atwood, "Validation by Holiness or Sovereignty: Religious Toleration as Political Theology in the Mongol World Empire of the Thirteenth Century," *The International History Review* 26, no. 2 (2004): 237–56.

[85] Timothy May, "Spilled Blood: Conflict and Culture over Animal Slaughter in Mongol Eurasia," in *Animals and Human Society in Asia: Historical and Ethical Perspectives*, ed. Rotem Kowner, Guy Bar-Oz, Michal Biran, Meir Shahar, and Gideon Shelach (New York: Palgrave Macmillan, 2019), forthcoming.

[86] Juvaini, trans. Boyle, 272.

[87] Juvaini, trans. Boyle, 214.

Chapter 5

With Success Comes Failure

A quick glance at the world map clearly indicates that the Mongol Empire no longer exists. Yet when did it end? The last Chinggisid ruler abdicated his throne in Khiva in 1920. Yet, one could hardly say the Khanate of Khiva was the last edifice of the Mongol Empire? Do we take 1260 as the end of empire, after the death of Möngke and the beginning of the civil war between Ariq Böke and Qubilai? As we've seen, this war did not strengthen the empire but fractured it into four or five separate states, with Qubilai's Yuan Empire having only a hypothetical sovereignty over the others. Or do we end it in 1305 with the end of the *Pax Mongolica*? As the Da Yuan Empire in East Asia was seen (at least by its rulers) as simply a Chinese term for the *Yeke Monggol Ulus*, do we assign the end of the empire to 1368 when the Mongols were driven out of China or in 1388, when the Northern Yuan ended?[88] Yet, the Jochid Ulus and Chaghatayids continued to rule, but even they did not end with a clear expiration date. Indeed, one can argue that the Mongol Empire never fell—it was never toppled by outside forces or natural disaster. Rather, it just faded away, slowly dissolving as a series of successor states emerged in its former territories as the Chinggisids gradually lost real authority even while their charisma still lingered.

In 1256, there was no reason to think the Mongol Empire would end. Not only were the Mongol armies once again on the move, but their ruler, Möngke was energetic—not only did he have a solid military reputation, but he also aggressively reformed the administration of the empire, rooting out corruption and increasing the centralization of the state. Indeed, his policies should have ensured the continuation of the empire rather than initiate its decline. Unfortunately, the seeds for the dissolution of the empire had been planted long before the Toluid Revolution and Möngke's reign.

As with the success of the Mongols, there is no single reason for its demise. Problems with succession, territorial issues, environmental factors, religion, disease, and the failure of Chinggis Khan's meritocratic system all factored into the decline of the Mongols. I will analyse each of them now in turn. One item, however, did *not* play a role—failure of the Mongol military. Although the Mamluks prevented the Mongol conquest of Syria and the Mongols failed in Japan, one would be hard pressed to say that the Mongol military had lost its edge. Indeed, the post-dissolution period shows that the Mongol military only became more adaptable and flexible in warfare. The key issue, however, was that Mongol armies spent more time fighting other Mongol armies than they did against foreign opponents. This is not to diminish the success of the Mamluks or samurai, or opponents in Southeast Asia. There were still enough Mongol successes to demonstrate that the Mongol style of warfare was still effective if not for other factors, often environmental, that were beyond their control. Indeed, one only had to look at the conquests of Tamerlane to see that with proper leadership, the Mongol military system remained successful.

Problems with Succession

A major issue in the decline were difficulties in succession. There was no clear system of succession among the Mongols except *tanistry*, which according to Joseph Fletcher was based largely on whomever could seize and hold the throne.[89] While Fletcher's observation has some merit, it was not quite that simple. While the youngest son by the senior wife inherited the household of the father, ultimogeniture did not necessarily indicate succession to the throne. Nor did primogeniture.

It is clear that Güyük favoured it, but it was not systematic. In previous steppe empires, lateral succession between brothers or even uncles occurred. Thus, any male blood relation of Chinggis Khan had a claim to the throne, at least hypothetically. Although Chinggis Khan named his heir, Ögödei, the Mongols failed to follow through with this practice. The system however was refined over time so that the only legitimate contenders were descended from Börte's sons. Although the Ögödeids declared that only they could rule as *khaghan*, it is not certain if this was simply their perspective or Chinggis Khan's decree. The purge that followed the Toluid Revolution that brought Möngke to the throne might suggest that perhaps the Ögödeid claim was genuine.

After the purge, no one considered the Ögödeids as a contender for the *khaghan's* throne again. Indeed, the strongest contender, Qaidu, never claimed the title for himself. His growing power, including dominance over the Chaghatayids, raised concerns among others, so much so that only his death in 1301 prevented an alliance between the Yuan, Jochids, and Ilkhanate against him.[90] To be certain a few Ögödeids reappeared later as puppet khans but, after Qaidu, the Ögödeids lacked a true leader to reestablish their claims. Qaidu's own offspring engaged in internecine warfare that not only thwarted them from dominating the Chaghatayids, but actually allowed the Chaghatayids to defeat and incorporate the Ögödeids. The Jochids and Yuan followed suit, seizing Ögödeid territory near their borders.

Let us consider the four later Mongol states in turn: the Yuan Empire, the Ilkhanate, the Chaghatayids, and the Jochids. Among the Yuan, one had to be a descendent of Qubilai to be a legitimate successor. As Qubilai outlived his own chosen heir, Jingim, Qubilai's grandson Temür Öljeitü became the next ruler. He died without sons however, which quickly reinstated the concept of *tanistry*. Whoever had the largest army and reached Daidu first tended to have the claim to the throne.

For the Ilkhanate, *tanistry* still applied but the only legitimate contenders came from the heirs of Hülegü, although those from the second Ilkhan, Abaqa, seemed to have the most success. Thus, the scramble for the throne and some-times brief civil wars tended to occur between uncle and nephew.[91] Curiously, a key reason for the decline of the Ilkhanate was a shortage of Hülegüids. For a short period, Arpa Ke'ün (r.1335–1336), a descendent of Ariq Böke was the nominal Ilkhan. He proved himself in battle, driving back the Jochids. He lacked sufficient support to impose his will on the rest of the khanate for reasons that will be explained later. As a result, the Ilkhanate fragmented into a number of successor states led not by Chinggisids, but rather the heirs of their generals.

The Chaghatayids faced similar problems. While they could rarely agree upon which Chaghatayid should sit on the throne, the Chaghatayids all agreed that they had enough of Ögödeid dominance after Qaidu. Once they ended the Ögödeid threat, the Chaghatayids settled into war amongst themselves. While some rulers did have respectably lengthy reigns with impressive achievements, events indicate that the Chaghatayid realm was not peaceful. While Almaliq became a capital, some Chaghatayids preferred residing in Bukhara and Qarshi. A growing divide between the eastern and western halves of the empire arose. It is not clear if this bifurcation was similar to the White and Blue halves of the Jochid (described in the next paragraph) or if it was accidental. Regardless, the fissiparous nature of the Chaghatayids became increasingly apparent.

The Jochids were not immune to this development either. Jochi left behind numerous sons, roughly forty. We know only fourteen by name.[92] The sons from his senior wife, Begtütmish, did not appear to have priority. Indeed, it is unclear if she produced any sons for Jochi. Although Batu may be considered the first Jochid Khan, Batuid descent did not guarantee the throne. Batu's brother Berke was the fourth Jochid ruler, as Batu's son and grandson both died in quick succession on the throne. Berke was unable to institute his own dynasty so the throne passed back and forth between Batuids and occasionally to the houses of other sons. Complicating matters was that the eastern portion of the Jochid

Khanate was the Blue Horde (Köke Orda) ruled by Orda (the eldest son of Jochi) and his heirs. While nominally subordinate to the western or White Horde (Aq Orda), there were periods in the fourteenth century when it was truly independent. Yet, it too faced succession issues when the line of another son of Jochi took the throne. Indeed, due to the sheer number of Jochids, during the mid-fourteenth century there were periods when multiple khans all vied for the throne in Sarai, the Jochid capital. Needless to say, the conflict over the throne distracted Jochid attention from affairs of state as well as their borders.

Territorial Issues

A key component to the dissolution of the Mongol Empire that directly affected succession matters was the appanage system and distribution of territory. As indicated earlier, Chinggis Khan provided each of his sons an appanage or allotment of territory. The original borders are vague, but they became more defined over time. While Chinggis Khan's brothers received Manchuria, Tolui received eastern Mongolia. Western Mongolia, particularly around the Orkhon Valley was imperial or *dalay* lands. Ögödei's territory extended from the Altai to perhaps Lake Balkhash and Chaghatayids ranged from the Amu Darya to the Tien Shan Mountains. Jochi's appanage was originally from the Irtysh River to the Volga River with a vague understanding that it also extended "as far in that direction as the hoof of the Tartar horse had penetrated."[93] The territory of those who submitted to the Mongols remained outside their appanages, such (at least initially) as the Tangut and Uighurs. With the rise of Ögödei, this may have changed with the Xi Xia being assigned to his son Köten and western Mongolia being viewed as Ögödeid territory. The western campaigns greatly extended the Jochids' realm to the Carpathians Mountains. Other territories were not assigned. Most of the early divisions appear to have been pastureland. The sedentary realms were conquered and made *dalay* lands, although the *altan urugh* also received *qubi* or shared territory. Again, they did not rule it directly, but rather received income from it so that Batu might receive revenues from a workshop in China and the sons of Ögödei received revenue from Tibet. Fiscal districts administered by the central government were also created to provide the state revenue. These consisted of North China, Turkistan (the caravan cities), and Khurāsān-Mazandaran. The remaining territory was occupied by the *tamma* armies. As the regions stabilized, the army was meant to move to the frontier and conquer more territory.[94]

Occasionally, the assignment and allocations of troops did not go as planned. As indicated previously, occasionally *tamma*s remained in a place for years and even decades. While Chormaqan's *tamma* is a successful example of what I have called the *tsunami* strategy and then the transition from military to civil authority, another *tamma* shows the reverse. When Chormaqan invaded the Middle East in the 1230s, he dispatched his lieutenant Dayir into present-day Afghanistan. Dayir's command became a separate *tamma.* Technically, he remained subordinate to Chormaqan, but time and distance made his *tamma* a separate command both on paper and in reality. After Dayir died, new commanders with reinforcements were dispatched.[95] A civil government never truly extended into the region. While Khurāsān transitioned into a province with an imperial civil authority, the regions of Ghazna, Ghūr, and Zābulistān never did. The *tammachi* there remained largely independent and operated under his own authority. These troops also raided into India frequently carrying back not only loot but also slaves, including women. Gradually, these Mongol troops became known as the *Qara'unas,* a term that still has not been adequately explained.[96] During Hülegü's Middle Eastern conquests, they were ostensibly under his command, but later actions proved that to be false. Indeed, in the late-thirteenth century, the *Qara'unas* proved to be independent and dangerous. Only in the early fourteenth century did they truly become subordinate to the Chaghatayid Khanate. Even then, they proved unreliable, as the forces that challenged Chaghatayid authority in Māwarānnahr originated from the *Qara'unas*. They also then became a key element in Tamerlane's armies.

The *tammachin* or commanders of the *tamma* often had close ties to the royal houses. For instance, Baiju, a Jochid commander, replaced Chormaqan in Azerbaijan. Although he accompanied Chormaqan in the original conquests, he still maintained his ties and loyalties with the Jochids. As the Jochids claimed Azerbaijan, Güyük may have attempted to curb those assertions by replacing Baiju with Eljigidei, but it is not certain. We do know that by the time of Möngke's reign, Batu was recognized as the major power in Azerbaijan, Georgia, and much of Iran. This may have also been a reward for his support of Möngke.

It is equally possible that Möngke dispatched Hülegü to the Middle East to curtail Jochid claims. Hülegü was sent after Batu's death and Möngke must have had some concerns as at least half of his empire was hypothetically under Jochid authority. This could not have sat well with him. Whatever Möngke's intent was, it remains speculation as Hülegü did not make any overt moves to claim from Amu Darya to the Euphrates until after Möngke's death. Meanwhile in China, it is equally uncertain if he intended to conquer the Song Empire and turn it into an appanage for Qubilai. If he did, it made sense. While the Song Empire lacked pasture, Qubilai's first conquest was Yunnan, outside of the Chinese orbit, but neighbouring it. Furthermore, it had suitable pasture for horses as well as extending the Toluid sphere. The question is how much of the southern territories did he intend for Qubilai?

This was a key issue and shows how the different geography of new territories became problematic. Previously the appanages were in steppe zones. The new conquests in the Middle East and China were not, although some small steppe areas did exist and could accommodate pastoral nomadism. With the exception of Hungary and the plains of Poland, the conquest of Europe would not have added any additional steppe lands either. Thus if the Mongols followed previous policy, the newly conquered lands would have been divided into *dalay* and *qubi*. Although the *altan urugh* continued to increase, no new appanages were forthcoming. This meant that lesser princes (sons of concubines and low-ranking wives) were unlikely to receive their own appanages, making them dependent on higher-ranking sons, unless additional territory could be gained. Furthermore, the attachment to territory in the sedentary realms also went against the normal nomadic view of empire—controlling people over territory.

Hülegü's appearance in western Iran and Azerbaijan was viewed as an intrusion on Jochid prerogatives. Berke could do little during Möngke's lifetime, but after the *khaghan*'s death, war broke out. Again, we do not know what Möngke's intention for Hülegü was, but Hülegü's position as a viceroy in the Middle East effectively placed a Toluid near Chaghatayid territory as well as closer to Sarai. Furthermore, it would deprive the Jochids of additional territory while improving the Toluid position. For the Jochids, retaining Azerbaijan was crucial not only for their own security, but also for further expansion. Preoccupation with reclaiming Azerbaijan distracted them from invading Central Europe. While raiding occurred, the Jochids made no effort to conquer Europe.

One of the most damaging aspects of the Toluid Revolution was the reduction of the Ögödeid *ulus*. While not all of it was confiscated, it was greatly reduced. Thus, even those Ögödeids who survived the war with the Song would not have the pastures or flocks and herds that could support a large retinue of nomads, thus putting them at a severe disadvantage compared to the other families. This also factored into Qaidu's career. The Chaghatayids also sought to expand at the expense of the new Ilkhanate. During the rise of Qaidu, the Chaghatayid Baraq was forced to renounce Chaghatayid claims to former Ögödeid territory. His compensation was to conquer territory in Khurāsān, including Herat. Baraq found the Ilkhan Abaqa less accommodating as the Ilkhan crushed the Chaghatayid forces at Herat in 1270. Afterwards Qaidu raised a more compliant (yet, no pawn) Chaghatayid to the throne in Du'a, who aided Qaidu in encroaching on Yuan territory in modern Xinjiang and even western Mongolia.

Qubilai still attempted to expand in Japan, Southeast Asia, and modern Indonesia, but none of these efforts were directly connected with acquiring territory for his sons and relatives. His failed efforts were tied to the concept of Mongol legitimacy and Tengri's will, but they were also tied to the restoration of the tribute system that was important to his legitimacy as a Chinese emperor. When he failed in his conquests, Qubilai was seen to have failed as the Khaghan of the Mongol Empire and thus did not inspire legitimacy among those outside of the Yuan, except for the Ilkhans who maintained token recognition. While his conquests failed in Japan, military actions in modern Vietnam, Cambodia, and Myanmar caused enough damage that those kingdoms acquiesced to paying tribute in order to prevent further Mongol incursions. Even a doomed effort with Indonesia returned with sufficient plunder that it could be rationalized as tribute. Most importantly, however, the Mongol efforts in Southeast Asia established new trade links and the wealth from the sea trade compensated for the lack of conquests.

Religion and Identity

Identity was a third factor in the decline of the Mongols. When Chinggis Khan founded the *Yeke Monggol Ulus* the defeated tribes were incorporated into the decimal units commanded by Mongol commanders. The intent was to forge a new identity, a Mongol one. In this, he was largely successful. Indeed, without Chinggis Khan it is questionable if there would be a people known as the Mongols today. Yet, he was not completely successful. Initially, he attempted to force sedentary groups into this identity before he learned that forcing an alien culture onto another was not practical.[97] Thereafter, the Mongol identity was reserved for the nomadic population. Those nomads that submitted became Mongol, adopting Mongol culture and customs. Overall, this was not a difficult transition as most of the other nomads were Turks who shared many customs and practices. While the Turkic languages are different from Mongolian, they share many commonalities in grammatical structure as well as loan words. Shared language, however, was not the key element in identity.

During the height of the Mongol Empire, this worked. By the late-thirteenth century, divisions in identity began to arise. While the *altan urugh* still promoted Mongolian unity through connection to Chinggis Khan, the divided empire could not retain a single identity. New identities began to emerge based on locality and regional influences. In the east, Qubilai and subsequent khans tried to balance their Mongol identity with also being a Chinese emperor. While it was previously believed that the Mongols wanted to prevent being assimilated by the Chinese, it is clear that Qubilai took steps to prevent the Chinese from becoming Mongols, as it would open the door to high rank and privileges.[98] While Qubilai maintained the city of Shangdu to keep in touch with his Mongolness, his other actions made Mongols in Mongolia view him with suspicion. One must bear in mind that the Mongols of Mongolia were also the former supporters of Ariq Böke and thus had little reason to respect Qubilai's claims to legitimacy. His successors faced these issues as well—balancing the Mongol identity with ruling as a Confucian-style Chinese emperor in order to maintain legitimacy over the majority of the empire's population.

Let us now consider the identities of the four late Mongol states in turn: the Yuan Empire in the time of Qubilai Khan, then the Jochids, the Ilkhanate, and lastly the Chaghatayids. Buddhism had already entered the picture in Qubilai's time. His use of Buddhism came through his wife Chabi's influence. She introduced him to the Phagspa Lama who not only developed a new writing script (Phagspa) that was meant to unite the empire (it didn't), but also provided Qubilai with another tool for legitimacy. Buddhism offered another avenue to combine with the charisma of the bloodline. When all of the contenders were Chinggisids, other forms of legitimacy were needed. Buddhism, specifically Tibetan Buddhism, performed this service. As it was not a Chinese variant, it served as a counter to Chinese influences. Furthermore, through the Phagspa Lama and Buddhism, Qubilai could connect his legitimacy through Buddhist modes of authority, adding another layer to his legitimacy. His successors largely followed his example, although their devotion varied greatly. A drawback was that many Chinese viewed the Tibetan form of Buddhism, particularly Tantric varieties, as an aberration and foreign. While it benefitted the Yuan dynasty on one level, it did little to endear the Mongol rulers to the Chinese.

In the Jochid territories, similar changers were going on. The Jochids gradually adopted a new religion, but it was not the Christianity of their sedentary subjects, the Rus'. Rather, they adopted Islam. Although Berke was a Muslim since his youth, most of the Jochid Mongols did not convert until the early fourteenth century. Berke used his religion to help justify his wars against the Ilkhanate—a *jihad* against the infidel. Whether this was to convince himself or others is debatable. After him, however, came rulers who did not share his faith. The switch occurred, as it did among the rest of the Mongols, when the nomadic population began to convert. Conversion among the Mongols was rarely a top down process. Islam was present in the region—among the Bulgars in the upper Volga as well as the wealthy commercial centre of Khwārazm. Muslim merchants also served as missionaries. Compared to the more rigid orthodoxy of the Rus', syncretic forms of Islam, such as sufism, were more appealing and the grandeur of Islamic culture was quite evident compared to less sophisticated Rus'. Again, it formed another avenue of legitimacy and a method of bolstering identity. A larger issue for the Jochids, as it would take decades before Islam became the dominant religion, was the increasing Turkicization of the Mongols. Compared to the millions of Kipchak Turks and other varieties who lived in the Pontic and Caspian steppes, the Mongols were perhaps a few thousand. While Mongols dominated the throne, intermarriage with Turks gradually accelerated Turkicization. Mongolian continued to be used in official correspondence, but as the Mongolian script was adopted from Uighur (a Turkic language), it was easy enough to use it for Turkic languages as well. Indeed, before the fourteenth century, Turkic was already being used in the court and as a *lingua franca.* Gradually, the Mongols ceased to be known as Mongols but as Tatars, a name known prior to the arrival of the Mongols. Indeed, Tatar became synonymous with the Mongols of the Jochid regions even though Chinggisid rulers continued well into the eighteenth century.

The Ilkhans never lost their Mongol identity, but they too adopted Islam in fits and starts. Nonetheless, they were the first Mongol polity to adopt Islam as the state religion. Again, it only occurred by the third and fourth generations when sufficient Mongol population among the commoners had converted. Although Ghazan Khan receives the credit, Tegüder Ahmad was the first Muslim Ilkhan. The adoption of Islam as a state religion greatly affected the Ilkhanate. While Christians and Jews suffered some oppression, Buddhism disappeared within the empire. The Islamization provided the Mongols some legitimization, but due to their continued adherence to the *yasa,* more conservative Muslims tended to view the Mongols' devotion with a sceptical eye. Nonetheless, the Mongols did convert and found the religion not only useful spiritually but also politically, as the power of the religion combined with the legacy of Chinggis Khan served as a powerful symbol of authority across diverse groups inside and outside of the empire. Unlike many Islamic dynasties, they had no need to seek a patent from a Caliph legitimating their authority. Indeed, with the destruction of the Abbasid Caliphate, the Mongols also demonstrated that legitimacy flowed through them rather than an archaic position long past its prime.

The Chaghatayids were the last to adopt Islam. It gained traction in the west first, which is not surprising as it was the more Islamic part of their realm. Bukhara, prior to its sack by Chinggis Khan, had been one of the foremost centres of Islamic learning. During the fourteenth century, it was well on its way to returning to that status. The eastern region had a more diverse population of Christians, Buddhists, and even Manicheans. Not until the mid-fourteenth century conversion of Tughluq Temür (r. 1347–1363) did Islam become the state religion. Again, this had to do with the trend as the nomads slowly adopted Islam. Nonetheless, the eastern and western portions of their territory developed different identities. The western region had a greater sedentary focus, although numerous nomads still dwelled in Māwarānnahr. They gradually viewed themselves as the Chaghatayids and viewed the eastern Chaghatayids as *jetes* or bandits, not only because of their demands for tribute but their raids. The eastern Chaghatayids continued to view themselves as Chaghatayids, but also referred to themselves as *Moghuls,* the Persian term for Mongol. Indeed, the eastern realm was known as Moghulistan. The use of the term reveals much about their identity. While they still claimed their Mongol identity, they now used a Turkic language interlaced with Persian terminology. Like the Jochids, numerous Turks dwelled in the region and over time the Mongols Turkicized. Mongol tribal names existed, but often in a Turkicized form such as the Barulas becoming the Barlas, the tribe from which Tamerlane emerged.

Environmental Factors in the Decline

Environment had an impact on Mongol failures as well. The largest issue, as alluded to before, included the need for pasture. In order to maintain their nomadic and hence Mongolian identity, pasture was needed. A key issue to the end of Mongol expansion was the lack of pasture. The Ilkhans failed to occupy Syria over the long term due to insufficient pasture. Qubilai's campaigns also failed in part to this, forcing them to be reliant on infantry. Furthermore, the humidity of Southeast Asia also had deleterious effects on their horses as well as their bows. There also has been recent discussion on climatic factors playing a role in the Mongol withdrawal from Hungary. This, however, remains inconclusive.[99]

Other climatic factors played a role as well. The early Mongol Empire existed during a wet period, which meant that the steppes of Eurasia were lush. By the fourteenth century, this began to change. A drier period meant that the steppes did not recover as quickly from grazing.[100] While the Mongols did not experience the desiccation of the steppes, which was a common hypothesis in the early twentieth century, they also did not experience the devastating *zhud*s or ice storms that are seen in modern Mongolia today. Regardless, the weather changed sufficiently enough that the steppes did not recover as they once did, making it more difficult to sustain large flocks and herds, which also then impacted the human population growth. Data is difficult to find, but one must question whether or not possible decline in both animals and population affected the Yuan Empire, eliminating Mongolia as a reservoir for troops.

Disease

Disease is always a factor in history and often underappreciated. For the Mongols, the bubonic plague affected them just as much as it did the rest of Eurasia. While the focus of studies on the bubonic plague has been on Europe, scholars have increasingly paid attention to how it impacted Eurasia.

The origins of the plague remain a mystery, originating either in the steppes or in the Himalayan foothills around Yunnan. In either case, the bacteria travelled via the thriving trade routes within the Mongol Empire. Protected and linking populous centres that provided the disease with new transmitters who travelled long distances, it is no wonder that Bubonic plague spread swiftly. The disease, however, was an equal opportunity infector. Station in life, religion, occupation mattered not—all were susceptible. Nomads tended not to be infected as they generally lived in small groups and away from each other, limiting transmission, as opposed to the effect in urban centres. They were not immune though. All it took was for transmission via a fleabite, as the flea regurgitated the *Yersenia pestis* into its victim. As the medieval Mongols were not known for their hygiene, they were perfect targets. While individual nomadic families could avoid the plague, large congregations ranging from *quriltais*, armies, and of course the courts of the princes and trade centres offered the disease avenues to transmission even among the nomads.

Although bubonic plague is treatable today, prior to the development of antibiotics, the untreated disease had a sixty percent mortality rate. Thus, the Mongols lost high numbers. As the nomads already had a lower population than sedentary populations, they lacked the means to quickly replace those losses. The disease weakened the military and the leadership. Certainly, it affected the populations they ruled, but sixty million can recover faster than a population of just one million.

The disease did not remain confined to the Mongols. Once again, trade routes accelerated the spread. While we may dismiss the fanciful account of the Jochids launching infected bodies into the Genoese port of Kaffa in Crimea, nonetheless the Genoese did bring the disease from there to the Mediterranean world where it spread from port to port before reaching Italy. The Middle East received the disease not only from the Genoese ships, but also from the caravan routes that connected Iran and Syria. Death was everywhere. Each region experienced the disease differently, but there can be little doubt that it hastened the unravelling of the Mongol States, as afterwards there was an increase of chaotic periods and a loosening of Mongol rule over their subjects, all of which facilitated rebellion, not only among the subjects but challenges from other Chinggisids for the throne.

The Failure of Chinggis Khan's Meritocracy and the Rise of the *Qarachu*

An underappreciated aspect in the demise of the Mongol Empire was the failure of the meritocracy created by Chinggis Khan. No matter what era, no matter what group, once a group elevates their status, they have no desire to lose it, nor for their descendants. For instance, part of the American dream for parents is that their children do at least as well, if not better, than they did. The Mongols were no different. Chinggis Khan's success was, in many ways, tied to a social revolution. Although he came from an aristocratic background, his unconventional childhood ensured that he was not beholden to the rigidity of the aristocracy. While he had aristocratic supporters, many of his most important ones came from commoner families. He judged individuals based on talent and promoted on that qualification.

In doing so, he made a category of men who were loyal to him and to him alone. He valued their talents and rewarded them appropriately. This transformed his companions from *nökhöd* (companions and bondsmen) to *noyad* (commanders, though it eventually came to mean lord). During the unification of Mongolia, Chinggis Khan eradicated competing aristocracies so that a viable alternative to Chinggisid rule did not exist. These commanders, however, gradually transformed into an aristocracy. Ironically, some of the policies that Chinggis Khan implemented to reward his faithful followers are the very ones that created the aristocracy that doomed the Mongol Empire. He permitted the sons of the father to inherit positions and also receive the same privileges, which could include immunity from taxes and punishments.

On the surface, this was not a bad plan. One can look at the case of Sübedei. His son Uriyangqadai and his grandson, Aju, became generals who proved quite capable in their service to the Mongol khans. Indeed, Uriyangqadai led the conquest of Dali while Aju was crucial to the conquest of the Song Empire during Qubilai's reign. Furthermore, if they were not talented, they would not have led armies for long. There remained opportunities for the rise of talented individuals as well. Promotion did become more difficult, however, as the upper levels of non-Chinggisid society became dominated by the *qarachu* or the "Black Ones." Mongolian society was divided into two components—white boned and black boned. The white were the royalty (Chinggisids). Everyone else was considered black boned. Of course, a hierarchy also existed among the "black." The commanders who dominated the upper levels of the administration and military were the *qarachu*,[101] many of whom also married Chinggisid princesses and thus became *quda* (in-laws through marriage alliance) but also *güregen* or sons-in-laws.

During the *Yeke Monggol Ulus* period, the system worked fine and *qarachu* proved to be trusted allies and a balance to the desires of the Chinggisids when advising the *khaghan*. In the post-dissolution period, however, things went awry. With several states now ruled by Chinggisids, there were now fewer Chinggisids who took part in any regional *quriltai* that selected a new khan. Combined with fewer conquests and thus fewer avenues for success and promotion, the *qarachu* now developed an interest in promoting khans who secured their interests, which sometimes conflicted with the best interests of the state. Strong khans could play the various *qarachu* factions off of each other, but weak, and particularly younger khans, were malleable puppets. Increasing conflict arose rather peaceful elections through a *quriltai*. On one hand, competing Chinggisids sought the throne, but also the *qarachu* promoted certain contenders. Their importance cannot be overlooked. The role of Nawruz in Ghazan's success or Chuban's in Abu Sa'id's early reign reveals the strength of the *qarachu*. In the Jochid territories, the *qarachu* Mamai used a number of puppet khans while he ran the empire. Even the great Tamerlane, whose abilities rivalled Chinggis Khan, maintained the pretence of Chinggisid rule by using three willing puppets. On the surface, the Yuan Empire seems to be the exception, but even there, high-ranking Mongol nobles controlled who ruled. They simply hid their actions behind their positions in the government. The *qarachu* institution became ingrained in the successor states to the Mongols so that, even in the 1700s, the *qarachu* were influential in the Crimean Khanate.

The *qarachu* eventually began to rule directly. Mamai did briefly, but it led to a revolt by Moscow. When a Chinggisid returned to the throne (Toqtamysh), Moscow paid dearly, but they legitimated their revolt on the grounds that a non-Chinggisid sat on the throne. When the Ilkhanate ended in 1335, a number of successor states arose. These were led either by local dynasts who maintained their throne, or by members of the *qarachu* such as in the Jalayir and Chubanid states. In Mongolia, the Oirats emerged as a force to be reckoned with and even challenged the Chinggisids for primacy in Mongolia. A curious turn of events considering that the Oirat were a minor tribe in Siberia during Chinggis Khan's rise to power. Yet, they became a *quda* family when Chinggis Khan married his daughter to the son of the Oirat leader, Quduqa Beki. Using this position for leverage, the Oirats became a significant force throughout the Mongol Empire. While their influence was crushed in the Ilkhanate in the late-thirteenth century, in the east they only grew. Indeed, during the fifteenth century, the Ming worried more about the Oirat than the Mongols, particularly after the Oirat crushed the Ming at the battle of Tumu in 1449, capturing the Ming emperor. Even when the Oirat declined, a number of their commanders and other *qarachu* tribes coalesced to form the Zhungar confederation, which vied with the Russian Empire and the Qing Empire for dominance of Inner Asia.[102]

The rise of the *qarachu* created a viable alternative that could challenge the *altan urugh*. While the *qarachu* lacked the same gravitas, they could influence events and attempt to manage which Chinggisid sat on the throne, thus dictating policy. Only when a *qarachu* achieved unparalleled power could they truly establish a true dynasty, such as the Timurids who not only ruled an empire in Central Asia and Iran in the fifteenth century, but also formed the basis of the Mughal Empire in the sixteenth century. This is not to say the Chinggisids were without vigour. Indeed, the Chinggisid Shaybanid dynasty (the Uzbeks) drove the Timurids out of Central Asia. The problem is that the Chinggisids continued to fracture, forming more and more small states that rivalled each other. As a result, the Mongol Empire did not end, but continued to disintegrate until it simply ceased to exist. In its wake, however, a number of new states emerged, which sometimes linked themselves to the Chinggisid legacy, or if lacking that, by latching on to the allure of the *qarachu,* as it was the next best thing.

Having identified half-a-dozen key factors behind the decline of the Mongol Empire, now let us turn to its huge legacy to the world.

Notes

[88] Regarding Da Yuan, see Hodong Kim, "Was 'Da Yuan' a Chinese Dynasty?," *Journal of Song-Yuan Studies* 45 (2015): 279–305.

[89] Joseph Fletcher, "The Mongols: Ecological and Social Perspectives," *Harvard Journal of Asiatic Studies* 46, no. 1 (1986): 11–50, at 17.

[90] Rashīd al-Dīn, ed. Karīmī, 508–9, 678; Rashiduddin, trans. Thackston, 248, 332.

[91] Arghun rejected Tegüder's authority, Ghazan reluctantly acquiesced to Geikhatu and then rebelled against Baidu.

[92] Rashiduddin, trans. Thackston, 246.

[93] Juvaini, trans. Boyle, 42.

[94] Timothy May, "Mongol Conquest Strategy in the Middle East," in *The Mongols' Middle East: Continuity and Transformation in Ilkhanid Iran*, ed. Bruno De Nicola and Charles Melville (Leiden: Brill, 2016), 13–37.

[95] Rashīd al-Dīn, ed. Karīmī, 66, 416; Rashiduddin, trans. Thackston, 214, 340.

[96] Hirotoshi Shimo, "The Qarāūnās in the Historical Materials of the Īlkhanate," *The Memoirs of the Toyo Bunko* 33 (1977), 131–81; Jean Aubin, "L'ethnogénèse des Qaraunas," *Turcica* 1 (1969): 65–95.

[97] See May, "Spilled Blood," forthcoming.

[98] Rossabi, *Khubilai Khan*, 174.

[99] Ulf Büntgen and Nicola Di Cosmo, "Climatic and Environmental Aspects of the Mongol Withdrawal from Hungary in 1242 CE," *Scientific Reports* 6:25606; doi: 10.1038/srep25606 (2016): 1–9. For the rebuttal see Zsolt Pinke, Laslo Ferenczi, et al., "Climate of Doubt: A Re-evaluation of Büntgen and Di Cosmo's Environmental Hypothesis for the Mongol Withdrawal from Hungary, 1242 CE," *Science Reports* 7:12695; doi: 10.1038/s41598-017-12128-6 (2017).

[100] Neil Pederson, et al., "Pluvials, Droughts, the Mongol Empire, and Modern Mongolia," *Proceedings of the National Academy of Science* 111, no. 12 (March 25, 2014): 4375–79.

[101] See Uli Schamiloglu, "The *Qaraci* Beys of the Later Golden Horde: Notes on the Organization of the Mongol World Empire," *Archivum Eurasiae Medii Aevi* 4 (1984): 283–97.

[102] For more on the Oirats and their place in Central Eurasian history see Joo-Yup Lee, "Were the Historical Oirats 'Western Mongols'? An Examination of Their Uniqueness in Relation to the Mongols," *Études mongoles et sibériennes, centrasiatiques et tibétaines* 47 (2016); http://emscat.revues.org/2820 (accessed July 19, 2018).

Chapter 6

Legacy of the Mongols

The Mongol Empire marks the transition from the medieval world to the modern world. The post-Mongol world looked considerably different from when the Mongols first arrived on history's stage. This change included not only the political map of Europe, but also in terms of religion, culture, technology, and ideas are part of what I term the Chinggis Exchange. This diffusion had an impact in world history similar to Alfred Crosby's Columbian Exchange, albeit perhaps more subtle.[103] This impact can be seen in political geography, the religious map of the world, and trade and information networks across Eurasia and beyond.

The Impact on Political Geography Today

Starting with the political geography, the most notable change brought about by the Mongol Empire occurred in China. Rather than three empires, there was only one, the Ming Empire. The Ming Empire benefitted greatly from the Mongol Empire and in many ways can truly be considered a successor state, particularly in the early decades of its existence. The Ming Empire was notable for the inclusion of Yunnan (the former kingdom of Dali), which had previously never been part of a Chinese state. In the north, there was Mongolia—it was not simply the steppes, but viewed distinctly as the home of the Mongols, who were ruled by Chinggisid khans. Although they briefly experienced unity under Dayan

Khan, the Mongols once again fractured into a number of "tribes." The border, which fluctuated considerably, became fixed as the Ming constructed the Great Wall at huge cost. While the wall served as a defence against the Mongols, it was also intended to prevent Chinese from escaping to the freedom of the steppes as well as to demarcate the extent of Chinese territory.[104]

In Central Asia, by the sixteenth century the Uzbeks moved into Māwarānnahr and occupied what would become, in the twentieth century, Uzbekistan. In the meantime, their empire fragmented into a number of small states known variously as the Emirates or Khanates of Bukhara, Khiva, and Kokand. These lasted until their conquest by the Russian Empire in the nineteenth century. Further north, the Kazakh Khanate formed. It too fragmented into three separate polities due to internal issues as well as external pressure from the Oirats and then later from the Zhungar Empire.

The former Ilkhanate had initially split into a number of small kingdoms ruled by local dynasts and *qarachu*. These were then conquered by Tamerlane. His own empire was short-lived. The Timurid Empire had a brief, but culturally important, life in Central Asia and Eastern Iran. The western portions were lost early to competing Turkmen confederations known as the Kara and Aq Qoyunlu (Black and White sheep). The Aq Qoyunlu gained supremacy for a short period, but they too suffered from decline, particularly due to pressure from the nascent Ottoman Empire, which arose in the vacuum in Anatolia. By 1500, the Ottomans had secured their position in Anatolia as well as Europe. The Aq Qoyunlu were then swept away by another Turkmen confederation known as the Safavids, who were united under a millenarian strain of Shi'ism. The Safavids marched across Iran, sweeping away the remaining Timurid principalities. Much like China under the Ming, Iran under the Safavids formed not only a distinct cultural entity, but a territorial one as well. Concepts of Iran had existed before, but the Safavid state formed more or less in the same borders as the Ilkhanate, excluding Anatolia. Indeed, the border between Iran and Iraq

today is partially due to the conflict between two Mongol successors—the Ottomans and the Safavids. The Timurids, under
pressure from both Uzbeks and Safavids, however, found new
life under Babur, who established a state in Afghanistan and
northern India. Although Babur was a Timurid, the population
of India considered any force coming out of Central Asia to be
Mongols, hence Babur's empire became known to history as
the Mughal Empire.

In the former Jochid states, the so-called Golden Horde
splintered into the Great Horde, the Crimean Khanate, the
Kazan Khanate, the Astrakhan Khanate, and the Sibir Khanate
(from which we get Siberia), as well as the Noghai Horde. As
Moscow and Muscovy benefitted greatly during Mongol rule,
transforming from an unimportant village into a major town
and centre of power, it was best situated to take advantage
of the Mongol collapse. The khanates were conquered one by
one, with Kazan (1552) and Astrakhan (1556) falling to Ivan IV
(the Terrible). Sibir fell to Cossacks in 1598 as Muscovy began
its expansion eastward in pursuit of land, partially driven by
a lust for furs (known as Russian Gold by some), and a desire
to find a trade route to China. The last vestige of the Golden
Horde came under Russian control in 1789.

The Religious Map

Russian expansion, however, also demonstrated the religious
changes that the Mongols had wrought. While Ivan the Terrible's campaigns were for territory, on one level they were
also religious wars of Orthodox Christianity against Muslims.
When the Mongols invaded the Islamic World, it caused a cri-
sis, as Muslims feared they were the harbingers of apocalyptic doom. Then Muslims had to adjust to being ruled by infidels. Gradually, the Mongols converted to Islam, except those
in the Yuan Empire. There were exceptions such as Ananda,
the Muslim grandson of Qubilai Khan who allegedly converted
one hundred and fifty thousand of his soldiers.[105] In the Yuan,
the Mongols turned to Buddhism, specifically Tibetan forms
of Buddhism. Today, if one superimposed a map of the Mon-

gol Empire over a map of regions with religious majorities, it would match this division of the Mongol religious world.

In the Middle East, the continuation of Islam is not unexpected, but we see the growth of Twelver Shi'ism. Previously, this was not the dominate form of Shia Islam. The Mongols' destruction of the Nizari Ismailis (the Assassins), ended the "Sevener" form of Shi'ism as an acceptable form of Islam in Iran. It still thrived in what is now Lebanon, but it was largely confined there with small pockets in India and Central Asia. Although the Ilkhan Öljeitü converted to Shia Islam, others did not. Nonetheless, his conversion permitted its growth. The key moment was when the Safavids adopted it and, with the fervour of new converts, forcibly implanted the Twelver sect across Iran. This is why Iran has a Shia majority today, quite different from the year 1200.[106]

Islam also spread into Central Asia. While Māwarānnahr was largely Muslim prior to the Mongols, beyond the Syr Darya, this country was very much a mixed bag of pagans, Buddhists, Muslims, Christians, and even Manicheans. By the late 1300s, the Mongols adopted Islam. The other religions gradually faded away in the region.

Curiously, Buddhism declined in Mongolia with the collapse of the Yuan. During the sixteenth century, Buddhism experienced a renaissance under the Mongols, but with new forms of Tibetan Buddhism. Two Mongols in particular played key roles. Abatai Khan built the monastery of Erdene Zuu in 1585 on the ruins of Qaraqorum (which had by then been destroyed by the Ming) and Altan Khan (d. 1582), who transformed the leader of the Buddhist Gelugpa sect into the Dalai Lama. From that moment, various Mongol leaders assisted the position of the Dalai Lama, often serving as a military wing to enforce Gelugpa supremacy over other sects and making the Dalai Lama a theocratic ruler over Tibet. Buddhist missionaries assisted the conversion of the Mongols as well as suppressing shamanism in Mongolia. As a result, Mongolia firmly became part of the Buddhist world until the 1930s, when the Mongolian government (then communist) destroyed the Buddhist institutions, purging thousands of monks. Buddhism has returned, but so has shamanism, along with other religions competing for souls in democratic Mongolia.

Curiously, despite having a Christian presence at the onset of the Mongol Empire, Christianity dwindled in Asia because of the Mongols. With the conversion of the Ilkhanate to Islam, the Church of the East (Nestorians), Syriac, Armenian, and Georgian Christians all suffered from sporadic persecutions and they often lost influence in the court. Significantly, the Mongols themselves did not convert to those branches of Christianity. Similar things happened in Central Asia so that the Church of the East gradually faded into obscurity. Orthodoxy never appealed to the Mongols and it is unclear if Orthodox missionaries ever attempted to convert the Mongols. The papacy, however, did attempt to convert the Mongols. While they never succeeded in luring the Mongols away from shamanism, Islam, or Buddhism, the Catholics were quite successful in converting Nestorians (whether Mongol, Turk, or Alan) to the Roman Church. The church, however, never created an internal infrastructure to produce native priests, forcing it to remain dependent on Rome to replenish it with bishops and priests. Thus after the fall of the Yuan and the Ming Dynasty's xenophobic attitude, Christianity in China and Mongolia also faded away.

Trade and Information Networks Across Eurasia and Beyond

The Mongols were known for trade and during the periods of *Pax Mongolica* (pre-dissolution and the official *Pax Mongolica* 1301–1305); merchants of all sorts crisscrossed Eurasia and expanded the sea trade. It is because of the security the Mongols provided that Marco Polo and Ibn Battuta visited China and India. The disruption of this trade, particularly in luxury goods, by the dissolution of the empire had a great impact. Wars in the Chaghatayid Khanate frequently closed the caravan routes and hence why the sea trade between the Yuan and Ilkhanate became so important. Tamerlane's destruction of Sarai started to reroute the land routes through his empire, which again affected the routes when it too fractured. The price of luxury goods, particularly spices skyrocketed. As mentioned before, Muscovy's expansion was driven not only by religious and territorial ambitions, but also in search of new trade routes. Yet they were not the only ones. Christopher Columbus' voyages were meant to reach India and the court of the Khan in China—despite the fact that the Mongols had not ruled China for over a hundred years. The latter also indicates how information no longer flowed across what Eugene Anderson termed the Mongol Super Information Highway.[107]

To see the impact, one only needs to look at the Chinggis Exchange to see the difference. During the Mongol Empire, not only did Western Europeans become relatively well-informed of events in the distant east through travellers such as John of Plano Carpini, William of Rubruck, and Marco Polo, but there was a flow of missionaries, mercenaries, and merchants across the Mongol Empire. Genoese and Venetians vied for trading privileges in both the Ilkhanate and the Golden Horde. The Black Sea trade was possibly the most important commercial operation of the fourteenth-century world. Access to ports there allowed Europeans to enter the markets of Sarai as well as Tabriz and then beyond. Its importance only grew with the fall of Acre, the last great Crusader stronghold on the Levant coast in 1291. Access to the Ilkhanate remained possible through Cilicia and ports on the southern Anatolian ports, but the Black Sea's importance increased. No matter their occupation, these missionaries, merchants, and mercenaries all returned not only with goods from the Mongol Empire, but also what they saw.

In addition, populations moved across Eurasia. We of course know the Mongols moved craftsmen around the empire from the beginning in order to set up colonies such as Chinqai Balasaghun (Chinqai's City), which was essentially an industrial centre in Mongolia churning out goods and weapons for the Mongol Empire. Similar colonies also existed. Yet in addition to artisans and the nomadic population moving to occupy new territories in their empire, merchants, missionaries, and others also moved about the Mongol Empire and even beyond it. Thus in Tabriz, during the Ilkhanate, there existed a centre for artists with Chinese, Persians, Armenians, and Italians. The result of this was a shift in art. Persian art adopted new elements. The Italians brought home these influences. While the Mongols did not create the Renaissance, they indirectly influenced it. In China, the governing institutions of the Yuan were filled with "westerners" or Semuren (the round-eye people). These westerners were simply anyone west of China proper. Thus, Uighurs, Persians, Arabs, and even some Europeans such as Marco Polo worked side by side with Chinese. While animosity existed, particularly between Confucians and Muslims, there are plenty of examples where this was not a problem. Furthermore, the animosity appears to have been less sectarian in nature, but based on jostling for influence and positions. Nonetheless, Middle Eastern influences penetrated Chinese art as well.

Technology flowed east and west as well. It is curious that the wheelbarrow appeared in Europe at the time of the Mongol Empire, whereas it had existed in China since the Han Dynasty (206 BCE–220 CE). Arabic medical texts were translated into Chinese, and foodstuffs from across the empire criss-crossed the realm and were used in new ways—not only for culinary purposes but also medical. In the Ilkhanate, Chinese astronomers worked alongside the great Shia polymath Naṣīr al-Dīn Ṭūsī. In the Yuan Empire, Middle Eastern scholars worked under the patronage of the Yuan court.

Mercenaries played their role as well. The counter-weight trebuchet was brought to China by Persian engineers as part of Qubilai's efforts to conquer the Song Empire, although Marco Polo attempted to take credit for it.[108] Recipes for gunpowder also circulated outside of China, appearing in Europe not long after William of Rubruck returned. In the fourteenth century, European cannons bore a curious similarity in design to those found in the Yuan Empire, and not only in basic function. Military ideas also flowed alongside technology. Among the Rus', they abandoned their old forms of warfare, which had proven effective against Pechenegs and Kipchaks, and adopted the Mongols' style of warfare. While they did not become nomadic horse archers, the Rus' adopted lamellar armour for its effective defence against arrows and also adopted the bow as their primary weapon over lances. While their horsemanship could not compare with the Mongols, the Rus' transformed into an effective medium cavalry. Tactics used at the battle of Aljubarrota (1385) in Portugal bear striking resemblance to the Mongol art of war. Again, not every influence can be traced through the documents. It is possible that someone who had contact with the Mongol Empire imported the tactical ideas or perhaps even learned from reading the work of Friar John de Plano Carpini who made explicit recommendations to the Papacy on how to fight the Mongols.[109] While this is speculation and does not rule out independent development in Europe, it does demonstrate the possibility that this knowledge could be passed on.

The transmission of gunpowder technology, however, ultimately led to the demise of steppe warfare, although not immediately. Not until the sixteenth century did firearms become suitable for massed formations. While it was easier to train "musketeers" than horse-archers, the key was the development of cannon that could be easily transported. These could break up the masses of horse-archers and at a range that prevented the nomads from unleashing a rain of arrows on the artillery positions. Only then and in concert with cavalry, could sedentary armies begin to conquer the steppes. Interest in Mongol warfare only resurfaced after the carnage of World War I when military theorists such as Liddell-Hart, Guderian, and Tukhachevsky began to consider how to use tanks and airplanes to regain mobility in warfare and avoid the hell of trench warfare. Only by reconsidering the tactics of steppe warfare and the success of the Mongols did they make significant progress.

Conclusions

The legacy of the Mongols permeates world history as the existence of the empire shaped the political landscape of Eurasia. The diffusion of technology, ideas, people, and goods altered how the Eurasian world operated and viewed the world. Although one should never discount the unparalleled destruction brought by the Mongol conquests, one cannot ignore the Mongol achievements either. Whereas historians of the past dismissed them as having neither architecture nor philosophy, the Mongol Empire proved to be every bit as complex and complicated as any other empire in history. While outsiders may have dismissed the Mongols as infidels and barbarians, the writings of these observers belie their emotional responses as they scratched their head at female rule, the fact that so many foreigners served the Mongols, their bewildering military power, and the loyalty and devotion demonstrated by the Mongols to their khans. In many ways, the documentary evidence left to us by travellers and chroniclers are mirrors of the authors' society. While they both marvelled at and dismissed various aspects of the Mongols, their culture, and their empire, the medieval writers also noted that only if their own societies would adopt some of the features of the Mongols, then they would be better off—and not just to resist the Mongols. Unfortunately, the less pleasant aspects of the Mongols have permeated the modern consciousness even while retaining the awe of Chinggis Khan's success. Nonetheless, he still tends to be imagined as a harbinger of doom while in Mongolia he is viewed as the father of their country (and rightly so). While his career and the Mongol Empire itself is being reevaluated for its impact in history, I cannot shake the feeling that Chinggis Khan would not have minded being known as the harbinger of doom, or as one writer had him utter, "the punishment of god."[110]

Notes

103 See Alfred Crosby, *The Columbian Exchange: Biological and Cultural Consequences of 1492*, 30th Anniversary ed. (Westport: Praeger, 2003); Timothy May, *The Mongol Conquests in World History* (London: Reaktion, 2012).

104 Arthur Waldron, *The Great Wall of China: From History to Myth* (Cambridge: Cambridge University Press, 1990), *passim.*

105 Rashīd al-Dīn, ed. Karīmī, 673; Rashiduddin, trans. Thackston, 329.

106 "Sevener" and "Twelver" refer to the number of Imams that the branches recognize.

107 Eugene N. Anderson, *Food and Environment in Early and Medieval China* (Philadelphia: University of Pennsylvania Press, 2014), 181.

108 Polo, trans. Cliff, 128.

109 John of Plano Carpini in Dawson, *Mission*, 32–38.

110 Juvaini, trans. Boyle, 105. Regarding Da Yuan, see Hodong Kim, "Was 'Da Yuan' a Chinese Dynasty?," *Journal of Song-Yuan Studies* 45 (2015): 279–305.

Timeline

1160	Yesügei takes Börte as a wife.
1162	Temüjin (Chinggis Khan) is born.
1164	Mongol confederation defeated by Jin-Tatar alliance.
1187	Jamuqa defeats Temüjin at Dalan-baljut. Temüjin takes refuge in Jin Empire
1195	Temüjin returns to Mongolia.
1204	Mongols defeat the Naiman at Chakirmaut and unify Mongolia.
1205	Mongols begin to raid Xi Xia.
1206	Temüjin becomes Chinggis Khan at Quriltai.
1209	Mongols invade Xi Xia.
1210	Xi Xia submits to the Mongols.
1211	Chinggis Khan invades the Jin Empire.
1215	Zhongdu falls.
1218	Güchülüg killed; Qara Khitai submits to Jebe; caravan massacred at Otrar.
1219	Chinggis Khan marches on the Khwārazmian Empire.
1223	Battle of Kalka River.
1227	Chinggis Khan dies; Xi Xia destroyed.
1229	Ögödei becomes new *khaghan* of the *Yeke Monggol Ulus*.

1234	Jin Empire is destroyed.
1235–1236	Qaraqorum is built.
1236	Mongols attack Bulghar and Kipchaks
1238	Chormaqan invades Armenia and Georgia.
1239	Conquest of the Rus' completed.
1240–1241	Ögödei dies; Töregene becomes regent.
1241	Mongols invade Poland and Hungary
1242	Chaghadai dies.
1246	Güyük becomes ruler of the Mongol Empire.
1248	Güyük dies. Oghul Qaimish becomes regent.
1250	Toluid Revolution; Möngke becomes *khaghan* of the Mongol Empire.
1252	Ergene becomes regent of Chaghatayid Ulus.
1256	Major invasion of Song Empire begins; Batu dies; destruction of the Ismaili Assassins by Hülegü.
1258	Siege of Baghdad and fall of the Abbasid Caliphate.
1259	Möngke Khan dies.
1260	Dissolution of the Empire; Ariq Böke and Qubilai hold separate *quriltais* and become khan. Civil war begins; defeat at 'Ayn Jālūt.
1262	War with Golden Horde begins.
1264	Ariq Böke surrenders.
1265	Ariq Böke dies; Hülegü dies.
1266	Berke Khan dies.
1267	Daidu constructed; Phagspa Lama develops new universal writing script for the Yuan Empire.
1271	Qaidu is crowned as Khan; Chaghatayid Khanate is subordinate to Qaidu.
1274	First Mongol invasion of Japan.
1279	Song Empire conquered.
1281	Second Mongol invasion of Japan.

1282	Baraq's son Du'a becomes Chaghatayid Khan.
1284	Abaqa's son Arghun becomes Il-Khan.
1286	Third Mongol invasion of Japan is cancelled; Mongols invade Java.
1291	Baidu and Gaikhatu compete for throne; Gaikhatu becomes Il-khan.
1294	Qubilai Khan dies.
1295	Temür Öljeitü becomes Emperor of the Yuan Empire; Ghazan makes Il-Khanate an Islamic empire
1301	Yuan armies defeat Qaidu; Qaidu later dies.
1303	Du'a takes control of Ögödeid and Chaghatayid Khanates.
1304	Peace throughout the Mongol Empire—*Pax Mongolica*; Ghazan dies; Öljeitü becomes Il-khan.
1307	Temür Öljeitü dies.
1310	Öljeitü converts to Shia Islam.
1316	Öljeitü dies, Abu Sa'id becomes the ruler and Amir Choban serves as regent.
1335	Abu Sa'id dies; Ilkhanate ends in succession squabbles.
1332	Toghon Temür takes throne in Yuan Empire.
1340s	The Black Plague strikes.
1342	Janibeg becomes Khan of the Golden Horde.
1343	Janibeg attacks Tana after sectarian riots; attacks Kaffa; Kaffa becomes an epicentre of Black Plague.
1359	Berdibeg Khan assassinated; Golden Horde descends into civil war.
1368	Yuan driven out of China; establishment of the Ming Dynasty
1370	Timur (Tamerlane) assumes power in Māwarānnahr.
1370s	Ascension of the *qarachu* Mamai in the west.

1370s and 1380s	Timur conquers former Ilkhanid domains.
1378	Toqtamysh takes control of Blue Horde with assistance from Tamerlane.
1380	Mamai defeated by Dmitri Donskoi at Kulikovo; Toqtamysh defeats Mamai at Kalka River.
1387	Toqtamysh begins war with Timur (Tamerlane).
1388	Yuan Dynasty ends; Northern Yuan Dynasty begins.
1395	Timur invades Golden Horde; Battle of Terek River and sack of Sarai.
1400s	Period of civil wars in Mongolia.
1480	Ahmad Khan of Golden Horde defeated at the Battle of Ugra River.
1505	Golden Horde truly ends.

Mongol Rulers: The United Mongol Empire Period (1206–1260)

Name	Reign
Chinggis Khan (Temüjin)	1206–1227
Tolui (regent)	1227–1229
Ögödei Khan	1229–1241
Töregene (regent)	1241–1246
Güyük Khan	1246–1248
Oghul Qaimish (regent)	1248–1251
Möngke Khan	1251–1259
Ariq Böke Khan	1260–1264 (contested)
Qubilai Khan	1260–1264 (contested)

Glossary

Altan Urugh	The Golden Family, the family of Chinggis Khan.
Anda	A blood brother.
Atabeg	A non-relative and servitor who trains a prince to rule.
Dalay	Imperial lands or property.
Daruqachi	(pl. *daruqachin*)A governor or agent of the Mongol empire.
Gerege	Passport or tablet that gave individuals permission to use the *jam*. The material of the *gerege* indicated the privileges of the bearer. Also known as *paiza*.
Güregen	Son-in-law. Someone married to a Chinggisid princess.
Hoi-yin Irgen	The Forest People who dwelt north of Mongolia. *Irgen* was used to refer to any non-Mongol group.
Jam	The postal system of the Mongol Empire. Also known as *yam*.
Jarquchi (pl. *jarquchin*)	A judge.
Jete	A derogatory term used to describe the nomads of Moghulistan. It meant bandit. Also known as *chete*.

Jüyin	The tribes and other groups on the border of the Jin Empire that guarded the frontier.
Kara Kumiss	Black kumiss, or distilled kumiss.
Keshig	The body guard institution of the *khaghan*.
Keshigten	A member of the *keshig*.
Khaghan	Emperor.
Khan	King.
Köke Möngke Tengri	The Blue Eternal Sky, the primary god of the Mongols.
Kumiss	Also known as *airagh*, fermented mare's milk.
Minggan	A unit of one thousand.
Moghul	Persian word of Mongols. Referred to the nomads of the western Chaghatayid khanate.
Nökör (pl. *Nökhöd*)	A companion, bondsman.
Noyan (pl. *Noyad*)	Commander.
Ordo	Literally camp, but it also became the word for palace or court.
Ortoq	A commercial alliance between merchants and members of the *altan urugh*. The *altan urugh* invested in the *ortoq* merchant, giving them an advantage over other merchants.
Paiza	See *gerege*.
Pax Mongolica	The period of peace throughout the Mongol Empire from 1304–1307.
Qara'unas	Literally the "Black Ones". Originally a *tamma* stationed in Afghanistan that became increasing independent.
Qarachu	Literally the Black Ones, referring to commanders and others who had reached high status, just below the *altan urugh*.

Qubi	Share or portion. Usually revenues given to members of the *altan urugh* originating from outside their appanage.
Quda	In-law or someone connected through a marriage alliance.
Qulan	Wild donkey.
Quriltai	A meeting or congress of princes, commanders and other dignitaries.
Tamgha	Stamp or seal. Also referred to a five to ten percent tariff on all goods traded in the Mongol Empire.
Tamma	A special military force send to the frontier of the Mongol Empire. They were to expand Mongol territory and influence as necessary.
Tammachi (pl. *tammachin*)	The commander or member of a *tamma*.
Tanistry	The concept where the throne is held by whomever can seize it and hold it.
Tümen	A unit of ten thousand.
Ulus	Nation or people. It transformed into also meaning appanage, patrimony, or state.
Yam	See *jam*.
Yasa	The body of laws within the Mongol Empire.
Yeke Monggol Ulus	The Great Mongol Nation or State. The Mongol Empire.
Zhud	A devastating storm, usually of ice and snow that kills livestock and also prevents animals from accessing pasture.

Further Reading

Primary Sources

Several primary sources here are cited in the footnotes, indicated mostly by the first part of the historical author's name below and the translator's surname.

Bar Hebraeus. *The Chronography of Abu'l Faraj*. Vol. 1. Translated by Ernest W. Wallis Budge. Piscataway: Gorgias, 2003.

> Bar Hebraeus, also known as Abu'l Faraj, witnessed the Mongol invasions of the Middle East and then also received patronage from Hülegü and other Ilkhans. His history begins in the Biblical era and extends well beyond his death to approximately 1295 providing a fascinating account of Ilkhanid rule from an Eastern Christian perspective. It can also be found at https://archive.org/download/Bar-HebraeusChronography.

Bar Sauma. *The History of Yaballaha III Nestorian Patriarch and of His Vicar Bar Sauma*. Translated by James A. Montgomery. New York: Octagon, 1966.

> Bar Sauma travelled from China to the Middle East on pilgrimage. His travelling companion, Markus, became Yaballaha III, Patriarch of the Church of the East. Bar Sauma, however, continued on to Europe as an emissary for the Ilkhanate. This is one of the few Eastern accounts of Europe, in effect a reverse Marco Polo.

Dawson, Christopher, ed. *Mission to Asia*. Toronto: University of Toronto Press, 1980.

> *Mission to Asia* is a crucial collection of translated accounts from Franciscan friars including John of Plano Carpini, William of Rubruck,

and John of Monte Corvino. All are excellent accounts of Europe's encounters with the Mongols. Additionally, this volume has correspondence between Güyük Khan and Pope Innocent IV.

Juvaini, Ata-Malik. *Genghis Khan: The History of the World-Conqueror.* Translated by J. A. Boyle. Seattle: University of Washington Press, 1997.

Juvaini, who held a position in Hülegü's government, provides a history of Mongols from the Mongol invasion of Central Asia to Hülegü's invasion of Iran, ending before the sack of Baghdad. The work is especially important for its coverage of the Khwārazmian Empire and Qara Khitai.

Odoric of Pordenone, *The Travels of Friar Odoric.* Translated by Sir Henry Yule. Grand Rapids: Eerdmans, 2002.

Like other Franciscan friars, Odoric sought to convert the Khan. His arrival in China did not achieve this, but his travel account provides a fascinating account of the late Yuan Empire.

Polo, Marco. *The Description of the World.* Translated by Sharon Kinoshita. Indianapolis: Hackett, 2016.

New documents and archaeology continue to demonstrate the value of Marco Polo's account of his time in the Mongol Empire. Kinoshita's excellent translation provides the flavour of the period and the accuracy that any reader could want.

——. *The Travels.* Translated by Nigel Cliff. New York: Penguin, 2015.

As several manuscripts of Marco Polo exist, it is always useful to read other translations. Cliff's translation compares favourably with Kinoshita's while making use of the other manuscripts.

Rashiduddin Fazlullah. *Jami'u't-Tawarikh: Compendium of Chronicles (Tome 1).* Translated by Wheeler M. Thackston. London: I. B. Tauris, 2012.

The third volume of Wheeler Thackston's translation of Persian histories dealing with the Mongols, Rashīd al-Dīn's (Rashiduddin) *Jami'u't-Tawarikh* is one of the first attempts at a world history. Making use of his position within the government and access to Mongol officials, Rashīd al-Dīn's work is indispensable for the study of the Mongols.

Takezaki Suenaga. In Little Need of Divine Intervention: Takezaki Suenaga's Scrolls of the Mongol Invasions of Japan. Translated byThomas D. Conlan. Ithaca: Cornell University East Asia Program, 2001.

Translation of the scrolls and other records related to the Mongol invasions. The book is bound so that it is to be read from right to left as that is how the scrolls were written and illustrated. Conlan's essay provides the appropriate context to appreciate the nuances of the work. Conlan argues convincingly that Japan would have been difficult to conquer even if the *tsunamis* had not occurred.

The Secret History of the Mongols. Edited and Translated by Igor de Rachwiltz. 3 vols. Leiden: Brill, 2004.

The best translation of the *Secret History of the Mongols* which is our most valuable source for the early life of Chinggis Khan. Most of the first two volumes are notes to the text. The third volume consists of additional notes and corrections. Indispensable for serious study of the empire. An open access version with minimal notes can be found here: https://cedar.wwu.edu/cedarbooks/4/.

Thomas of Split. *History of the Bishops and Salona and Split.* Translated and edited by Damir Karbic, Mirjana Matijevic, and James Ross Sweeney. New York: Central European University Press, 2006.

Thomas of Split was a witness to the Mongol invasion of Hungary. His work is particularly valuable as it provides extensive details of Hungarian history prior and after the invasion. The book is arranged with the Latin text on one page and the English translation on the opposite.

William of Rubruck. *The Mission of Friar of William of Rubruck: His Journey to the Court of the Great Khan Möngke, 1253-1255.* Translated by Peter Jackson. Indianapolis: Hackett, 2009.

The best translation of William of Rubruck. The footnotes and commentary by Peter Jackson add to the value of this work.

Zenkovksy, Serge A., ed. *The Nikonian Chronicle.* 5 vols. Translated by Serge A. Zenkovsky and Betty Jean Zenkovsky. Princeton: Kingston, 1986.

An accessible translation of the *Chronicle of Nikon.* It provides the long-term perspective of interactions between the Rus' and the Mongols as well as events on the periphery of this relationship. Invaluable for studying the Golden Horde.

Secondary Sources

Allsen, Thomas T. *Commodity and Exchange in the Mongol Empire.* Cambridge: Cambridge University Press, 1997.

> Examines the importance of Islamic textiles, particularly *nasij,* or gold brocade within the Mongol Empire. Allsen's work highlights themes within the empire beyond the typical focus on military actions and government institutions.

——.*Culture and Conquest in Mongol Eurasia.* Cambridge: Cambridge University Press, 2001.

> One of the first studies to establish how the Mongols' transcontinental empire served not only to promote trade, but also disseminate new ideas and trade. Furthermore, Allsen demonstrates that the Mongols were active participants in this exchange of goods and ideas.

——.*Mongol Imperialism: The Policies of Grand Qan Möngke in China, Russia, and the Islamic Lands, 1251–1259.* Berkeley: University of California Press, 1987.

> Allsen's first book and it remains one of the most important studies of the Mongol Empire. Allsen's groundbreaking study sheds light not only how the Mongol Empire operated but how it changed, demonstrating that the Mongols operated with a complexity previously not appreciated.

Amitai-Preiss, Reuven. *Mongols and Mamluks: The Mamluk-Ilkhānid war, 1260–1281.* Cambridge: Cambridge University Press, 1995.

> The first major study of the conflict between the Mongol Ilkhanate and the Mamluk Sultanate beyond individual battles. This work also demonstrates the value of the Arabic sources to the study of the Mongol Empire.

Atwood, Christopher P. *Encyclopedia of Mongolia and the Mongol Empire.* New York: Facts on File, 2004.

> An impressive reference work. As the title indicates this is a work for not only the Mongolian Empire, but truly all things related to Mongolia. There is no other work with the same level of detail and insight.

Biran, Michal. *Chinggis Khan.* London: Oneworld, 2007.

> One of the best biographies of Chinggis Khan. Biran also focuses on how Chinggis Khan shaped the Islamic world.

Buell, Paul and Francesca Fiaschetti. *Historical Dictionary of the Mongol Empire*. 2nd ed. Lanham: Rowman & Littlefield, 2018.

> An updated version of Buell's first edition expanded and corrected. It remains an indispensable reference and includes essays outlining the history of the Mongol Empire and the successors khanates. The Yuan essay is of particular value. The first edition can be found in an affordable paper back: Buell, Paul. *The A to Z of the Mongol Empire.* Lanham: Scarecrow, 2010.

Broadbridge, Anne F. *Women and the Making of the Mongol Empire*. Cambridge: Cambridge University Press, 2018.

> A study of the Mongol Empire with an emphasis on the role of the Mongol queens, including the daughters of Chinggis Khan. One of the most important recent studies on the Mongol Empire.

De Nicola, Bruno. *Women in Mongol Iran, The Khātūns, 1206–1335.* Edinburgh: Edinburgh University Press, 2017.

> De Nicola investigates the role of the wives of the Ilkhans and their influence not only on society in the Ilkhanate but also their role in the politics and governing.

Dunnell, Ruth. *Chinggis Khan*. Boston: Pearson, 2010.

> The second of the recommended biographies of Chinggis Khan. Brief but informative and suitable for classroom use.

Halperin, Charles J. *The Tatar Yoke: The Image of the Mongols in Medieval Russia*. Corrected ed. Bloomington: Slavica, 2009.

> Originally published in 1985, Halperin demonstrates how the Orthodox bookmen altered historical records to obscure Rus' familiarity with the Mongols and created a narrative of oppressive rule and influence on Russia. An essential work for the study of the Golden Horde and for understanding the Rus' sources.

——. *Russia and the Mongol Horde: The Mongol Impact on Medieval Russian History.* Bloomington: Indiana University Press, 1987.

> Despite its age, it remains a key study for understanding Rus' and Mongol relations as well as serving as an introduction to the Golden Horde.

Haw, Stephen G. *Marco Polo's China: A Venetian in the realm of Khubilai Khan.* New York: Routledge, 2006.

> Haw convincingly argues that Marco Polo did indeed visit China and serve in the court of Qubilai Khan. The author's dissection of Polo's account also sheds light on many ubiquitous aspects of Yuan China.

Jackson, Peter. *The Mongols and the Islamic World from Conquest to Conversion*. New York: Columbia University Press, 2017.

> Jackson's *magnum opus*. In addition to the narrative of the Mongols interaction with the Islamic world, he explores their impact including their early destruction of much of Central Asia and the Middle East. Jackson also discusses how the Mongols conversion to Islam expanded and influenced the Islamic world, demonstrating the Mongols had as much an impact on Islam and it did on them.

——. *The Mongols and the West*, 2nd ed. Boston: Pearson, 2018.

> A masterful study of Mongol contact with Western Europe. Jackson explores not only the violent encounters, such as the invasion of the west and diplomatic efforts, but also how Western Europeans perceived the Mongols and how that influenced them.

May, Timothy. *The Mongol Art of War*. Barnsley: Pen & Sword, 2007 and 2016.

> *The Mongol Art of War* discusses the development and organization of the Mongol military.

——. *The Mongol Conquests in World History*. London: Reaktion, 2012.

> This work explores the impact of the Mongol expansion on world history with a particular emphasis on the Chinggis Exchange or the concept of transmission of goods, knowledge, and people across the empire and how it altered the world.

——. *The Mongol Empire*. Edinburgh: Edinburgh University Press, 2018.

> A narrative history of the Mongol Empire from its rise to the end of each of the successor khanates. It also explores the relationship of the Mongols with Islam exploring how it changed over time.

——. ed. *The Mongol Empire, A Historical Encyclopedia*. Santa Barbara: ABC-Clio, 2016.

> The third reference work on the Mongol Empire. It is organized by theme and also includes primary source selections.

Morgan, David. *The Mongols*. 2nd ed. Malden: Blackwell, 2007.

> Originally published in 1986, *The Mongols* long remained the standard introduction to the study of the Mongol Empire. The second edition adds a chapter on the historiography up to 2007. While outdated in some ways, it remains the best work in understanding the history of the study of the Mongol Empire.

Ostrowski, Donald. *Muscovy and the Mongols: Cross-Cultural Influences on the Steppe Frontier, 1304-1589.* Cambridge: Cambridge University Press, 1998.

> As the title suggest, *Muscovy and the Mongols* explores how the Mongols influenced Muscovy. Ostrowski differs somewhat from Halperin but they both agree that the "Mongol Yoke" was not quite how Russian historians have depicted it.

Ratchnevsky, Paul. *Genghis Khan, His Life and Legacy.* Translated by Thomas Nivison Haining. London: Blackwell, 1991.

> The third recommended biography of Chinggis Khan. It is the most detailed with an emphasis on Chinggis Khan's early life. The English translation differs from the original German as many of the detailed footnotes have been worked into the text providing additional detail without becoming tedious in scholarly apparatus.

Rossabi, Morris. *Khubilai Khan.* Berkeley: University of California Press, 2009.

> Originally published in 1988, Rossabi's biography of Qubilai Khan remains unsurpassed and will likely remain that way for decades. A masterful study that not only reconstructs Qubilai's life but also attempts to understand the influences and motives of one of the greatest rulers in history.

——. *Voyager from Xanadu: Rabban Sauma and the First Journey from China to the West.* Berkeley: University of California Press, 2010.

> Rossabi explores and discusses Rabban Sauma's journey. The book is more than a narrative account of the primary source as he explores and discusses the world of Rabban Sauma, elaborating the journey and providing context to Rabban Sauma's travel account.